INDUSTRIAL LAW NOTEBOOK

by

NORMAN M. SELWYN

LL.M., Dip.Econ.(Oxon.), F.C.C.S.
of Gray's Inn, Barrister-at-Law;
Lecturer in Law at the University of Aston in Birmingham

LONDON
BUTTERWORTHS
1970

ENGLAND:	BUTTERWORTH & CO. (PUBLISHERS) LTD.
	LONDON: 88 KINGSWAY, W.C.2
AUSTRALIA:	BUTTERWORTH & CO. (AUSTRALIA) LTD.
	SYDNEY: 20 LOFTUS STREET
	MELBOURNE: 343 LITTLE COLLINS STREET
	BRISBANE: 240 QUEEN STREET
CANADA:	BUTTERWORTH & CO. (CANADA) LTD.
	TORONTO: 14 CURITY AVENUE, 374
NEW ZEALAND:	BUTTERWORTH & CO. (NEW ZEALAND) LTD.
	WELLINGTON: 49–51 BALLANCE STREET
	AUCKLAND: 35 HIGH STREET
SOUTH AFRICA:	BUTTERWORTH & CO. (SOUTH AFRICA) LTD.
	DURBAN: 33–35 BEACH GROVE

©

BUTTERWORTH & CO. (PUBLISHERS) LTD.
1970

Standard Book Number: 406 65345 3

Printed in Great Britain by Page Bros. (Norwich) Ltd., Mile Cross Lane
Norwich

Preface

This book is designed to provide students with a short outline of the subject in concise note form. It is not intended to be a substitute for a text-book, but a revision aid.

Where statutory provisions are referred to, I have tried to simplify them by paraphrasing; it is hoped that accuracy has not suffered thereby. I have also covered most of the ground which students would normally expect to find in examinations.

I am grateful to my colleague Vincent Powell-Smith for placing his editorial experience at my disposal, but sins of omission and commission are my own responsibility.

N.M.S.

November 1969.

Contents

Chapter 1   *The Contract of Employment*

1. General

The law relating to the formation of the contract of employment is basically the same as the ordinary law of contract as applied to the particular situation, together with certain statutory provisions. For the principles of offer, acceptance, etc., the student should refer to a standard work on the subject. Here it is proposed to deal with those contractual provisions which are particularly appropriate to employment law.

2. The Parties to the Contract

It is necessary to distinguish between a contract of service, and a contract for services. The former gives rise to the relationship of employer/employee, the latter will result in an employer/independent contractor relationship.

(a) THE CONTROL TEST—The basic test to be applied is one of control. An employee is a person who is subject to the orders of his employer *as to the manner* in which the work shall be done: *Yewens* v. *Noakes* (1880). In other words, the employer can tell his employee not only *what* to do, but *how* to do it: *Performing Rights Society* v. *Mitchell and Booker* (1924).

(b) UNREALITY OF THE TEST—A major defect of this test is that it fails to meet modern conditions, in particular with regard to highly qualified persons who frequently know more about the job than their employers, e.g. accountants, lawyers, chemists, etc., who may still be "employed" persons. DENNING, L.J. suggested an "*organisational test*" in *Stevenson, Jordan and Harrison, Ltd.* v. *McDonald and Evans* (1952). "Under a contract of service, a man is employed as part of the business, and his work is done as an integral part of the business".

Other factors may have to be taken into account, e.g. how, and by whom, the employee is to be paid, the manner of hiring and dismissal, the nature of the work, etc.

Market Investigations, Ltd. v. *Ministry of Social Security* (1969)

A company employed women to do market research on a part-time basis.

Held, the right to control was evidence of service, but was not an essential part. The fundamental test is "Is the person who has engaged himself to perform these services performing them in business on his own account:" *per* COOKE, J. On the facts it was held that the women were employees of the company.

In *Ready Mixed Concrete (South East), Ltd.* v. *Ministry of Pensions* (1968) it was held that a contract of employment existed if:

   (i) the employee agreed that in consideration of a wage he will provide his own work and skill in the performance of some service for his employer;
  (ii) he agreed that in the performance of that service he would be subject to his employer's control;
 (iii) the other provisions of the contract are consistent with it being a contract of employment.

(c) IMPORTANCE OF THIS DISTINCTION—The reasons for stressing the distinction between an employee and an independent contractor are:

   (i) An employer does not need to stamp the insurance cards of an independent contractor, he need not deduct P.A.Y.E. and he is not required to pay S.E.T.
  (ii) The employer is not generally liable for the wrongful acts committed by an independent contractor during the course of the employment (see below) whereas he may be liable for identical acts committed by his employee.
 iii) The duties owed by an employer at common law to ensure

the safety of his employees (see below) are more stringent than those owed to an independent contractor: *Savory* v. *Holland* (1964).

(iv) An employee is entitled to receive written notice of his terms of employment under the Contracts of Employment Act 1963 (see below), to certain minimum period of notice on his dismissal, and (possibly) wages during sickness.

(v) An employee may be entitled to receive payments, in appropriate circumstances, under the Redundancy Payments Act 1965 (see below).

(vi) An employer may not bring an action against a person who induces his employees to break their contract of service in circumstances where the Trade Disputes Acts 1906–1965 apply (see below), but the inducement of a similar breach of a contract made between an employer and an independent contractor may be actionable: *Emerald Construction Co.* v. *Lothian* (1966).

(vii) An employer may reap the benefit of any invention made by his employee in the course of the employment (see below) but this rule does not apply to independent contractors.

(d) LOANED EMPLOYEES—There is a strong presumption against the transfer of an employee from his general employer to a temporary employer: *Chowhardy* v. *Gillot* (1947). It is essential that the right to control be transferred, and the consent of the employee be obtained: *Nokes* v. *Doncaster Amalgamated Collieries* (1940). It has been suggested that skilled men cannot be transferred, but unskilled men may be: *Denham* v. *Midland Employers' Mutual Insurance Co.* (1955).

It seems that if a loaned employee commits a wrongful act while he is working for his temporary employer, the general employer will still be liable.

Mersey Docks and Harbour Board v. *Coggin & Griffiths, Ltd.* (1946).

A firm of stevedores hired from the Board a crane and driver; a clause in the contract provided that the driver was to be the servant of the hirers. The driver continued to be paid by the Board, who alone could dismiss him. The driver injured someone through his negligence.

Held, the Board, as the general employer was liable for the wrongful act of the driver.

However, it is possible for the general employer to negate his liability by making an express provision in the contract to this effect.

Arthur White, Ltd. v. *Tarmac Civil Engineering, Ltd.* (1967)

The owners of a crane-excavator hired it, together with a driver to the respondents. The contract provided that the driver, shall for all purposes be regarded as the servant of the hirers, who alone were to be responsible for all claims arising in connection with the operation of the plant by the driver. Due to the latter's negligence, another employee was injured.

Held, the respondents were liable.

3. Formation of a Contract of Employment

A contract of employment can be in writing, or made orally. Under the Merchant Shipping Act 1894, employment contracts made by seamen must be in writing, and contracts for apprenticeships must be made by deed: Apprenticeship Act 1814. However, under the Contracts of Employment Act 1963, the employer must give, within 13 weeks of the commencement of the contract, a written statement to the employee containing the terms of employment. This must include:

(a) the date of the commencement of the employment;
(b) the rate of remuneration and when payable;
(c) the hours of work;
(d) holidays and holiday pay;
(e) sickness pay and pension schemes (if any);
(f) period of notice (see below).

Any change in these terms must be notified to the employee within one month. It is not necessary to provide these written terms if the employee is engaged under a written contract which already provides these details, or has access to, or a copy of, a document which contains the terms.

An employee who complains that he has not received such a statement, or that it is inaccurate or insufficient, may take the matter before the Industrial Tribunal, which will decide the issue, and its decision shall take effect as if it was included in the written statement issued by the employer.

Written particulars need not be given to

(a) employees who work less than 21 hours per week
(b) registered dock-workers
(c) certain marine workers and fisherman
(d) Crown employees
(e) employees who work mainly or wholly outside Great Britain
(f) certain relatives of an employer.

CAPACITY—is governed by the general law of contract, but we may note:

(a) Civil servants are employed at the Crown's pleasure, and can be dismissed without notice: *Riordan* v. *War Office* (1960).
(b) Infants are bound by contracts of service or apprenticeship if, on the whole, they are for the infants' benefit: *Doyle* v. *White City Stadium* (1935).

4. Covenants in Restraint of Trade

An employer may try to protect himself against future competition by his employee by making the latter sign a covenant imposing a restraint on his future conduct after leaving the employment. The employer may only do this successfully if he has some proprietory interest to protect, for he is not entitled to protect himself from the mere competition of the employee.

Strange, Ltd. v. *Mann* (1965)

The defendant was employed as the manager of a firm of bookmakers, and he covenanted that he would not, after leaving his employment, be engaged or interested in any similar business within a radius of twelve miles. Most of the betting was done by telephone. After leaving the employment, the defendant set up a similar business within the restricted area.

Held, the restriction was void. The defendant's position was not such that he was obtaining the goodwill of the customers, because he did not render any particular service to them. The covenant was designed to prevent legitimate competition, and purported to give the plaintiffs a protection to which they were not entitled.

The proprietory interests capable of being protected are:

(a) trade secrets (*Haynes* v. *Dorman* (1899)) but not special methods of organisation: *Herbert Morris, Ltd.* v. *Saxelby* (1916). But a covenant cannot be so framed as to prevent an employee from using his skill and knowledge, or deprive him of his right to work.

Commercial Plastics, Ltd. v. *Vincent* (1965)

The plaintiffs employed the defendant to work on their production of P.V.C. calendered sheeting for adhesive tape. Because of the confidential nature of the work, the defendant agreed not to seek employment with any competitors in the P.V.C. calendering field for one year after leaving his employment.

Held, the restriction was void. The protection required by the plaintiffs was only in respect of the production of sheeting for adhesive tape. The covenant, as drafted, extended to the whole field of calendered sheeting, and was, therefore, too wide.

(b) *Existing customers* (*Plowman* v. *Ash* (1964)) but not future or potential customers.

Gledhow Autoparts, Ltd. v. *Delaney* (1965)

The defendant was employed by the plaintiffs as a commercial traveller. He agreed that after leaving his employment, he would not seek orders from any firm within the districts in which he had operated.

Held, as the restraint extended to firms who were not necessarily customers of the plaintiffs, it was void.

To determine the validity of these restraints, the nature of the business must be examined, and the position of the employee in the firm taken into consideration. If there is little likelihood of recurrent business coming in from customers, a restraint will be bad: *Bowler* v. *Lovegrove* (1921). If there is a goodwill following, a restraint may be upheld: *Scorer* v. *Seymour Johns* (1966) An employee who does not come into contact with customers cannot be re-strained from approaching them (*Strange* v. *Mann* (1965)) nor can a greater restraint be imposed than is warranted by his position: *Atwood* v. *Lamont* (1920). In addition, a covenant will only be upheld by the courts if it is reasonable, and not too wide in terms of time and area.

Mason v. *Provident Supply Co.* (1913)

The plaintiff was employed as a canvasser for a firm of credit drapers. A covenant restraining him from being connected with any similar business within 25 miles radius of London was held to be too wide in these circumstances.

Herbert Morris v. *Saxelby* (1916)

A seven year restraint on an engineer was held to be void, for there were no trade secrets or customer connections to protect, and the only knowledge he had acquired was how to organise a department.

What is reasonable in terms of time and area restrictions must depend on the facts of each case.

Fitch v. *Dewes* (1921)

A solicitor's managing clerk was held to be bound by a restraint which prevented him from being employed within a radius of seven miles from Tamworth, even though it was for life.

Nordenfelt v. *Maxim Nordenfelt* (1894)

N., an inventor, sold his armanents business to a company, and undertook not to compete with the company anywhere in the world for 25 years. In view of the world wide nature of the business, and the consideration he had received for his promise, the restraint was upheld.

SEVERANCE—The courts will construe such covenants very strictly, and generally speaking they must stand or fall as they are. The court will not re-write the covenant for the parties, for the question is not whether they could have made a valid agreement, but whether the agreement as it stands is valid. However, the court may apply the "blue pencil" rule, i.e. strike out the terms which are too wide. If that which remains is valid, it will stand. Otherwise, the whole covenant is void.

Scorer v. *Seymour Johns* (1966)

The defendant was employed with a firm of estate agents in Kingsbridge, and he agreed not to engage himself in a similar capacity anfter leaving his employment within a radius of five miles from Kingsbridge and Dartmouth. The defendant was dismissed, and he opened up an office as an estate agent within 5 miles of Kingsbridge, though outside a five-mile radius from Dartmouth.
Held, the covenant was severable, and the restraint on practising within five miles of Kingsbridge could be upheld. The restraint in respect of Dartmouth, which was unreasonable, would be struck out.

An agreement between employers, whereby they undertake not to engage each other's ex-employees within a certain period may equally be void as being against public policy.

Kores Manufacturing Co. v. *Kolok Manufacturing Co.* (1959).
Two companies engaging in a similar business agreed not to employ any person who had been in the employ of the other company within the previous five years.
Held, the agreement was void. Had the restraint been imposed by one of the firms on its employees, it would clearly have been too wide. The parties to this agreement were trying to do in an indirect manner that which could not be done directly.

5. Duties of the Employee

The employee undertakes to serve his employer faithfully, and any act which is detrimental to the interests of the employer is a breach of that duty. Thus the employee undertakes:

(a) To do the work personally. An agreement whereby the employee has the right to use a substitute may indicate that he is an independent contractor: see *Ready Mixed Concrete* v. *Ministry of Pension* (1968).

(b) To obey all lawful and reasonable orders. (What is reasonable is a question of fact, see below.)

(c) Not to engage in any conduct which is contrary or detrimental to the employer's interest.

Pearce v. *Foster* (1886)

The plaintiff was employed as a confidential clerk to advise his employers on securities. It was then found that he was speculating on the Stock Exchange.

Held, the employers were entitled to dismiss him summarily. Because of his activities, he could not give objective and disinterested advice to his employers.

(d) To indemnify his employer if the employee's acts cause injury or damage to another person.

Lister v. *Romford Ice and Cold Storage Co.* (1957)

While reversing his lorry, L. knocked down and injured another employee. The latter obtained damages from his employers, who brought an action against L. to be indemnified for their loss.

Held, the action would succeed. It was an implied term of his contract that he would perform his duties with proper care, and the employers could recover for a breach of that term.

(e) Not to accept bribes or secret commissions, even if these in no way influence the employee, nor cause him to act contrary to the employer's interests.

Boston Deep Fishing and Ice Co. v. *Ansell* (1888)

The plaintiffs employed the defendant as a managing director. He was dismissed, and subsequently they discovered that he had been accepting a commission from various firms in connection with contracts placed by the company.

Held, the company had a legal right to discharge him for a breach of his duty of faithful service.

(f) To account to his employers for the benefits of any patent or discovery made during the course of his employment provided he was doing work he was employed to do, and using his employer's time and/or materials.

British Syphon Co. v. *Homewood* (1956)

The defendant, who was the chief technician to the plaintiffs, invented a soda water dispenser. He patented it in his own name, and started to work for a rival company.

Held, the patent must be held for the benefit of the plaintiffs.

The test in these cases is whether or not it would be a breach of his duty of faithful service to withhold the invention from the employer.

(g) Not to engage in competition with his employer or to utilise his time or energy so as to harm his employer's interests.

Hivac v. *Park Royal Scientific Instruments, Ltd.* (1946)

Employees of the plaintiffs worked for the defendants, a rival company, in their spare time.

Held, the employees were in breach of their contracts, and an injunction would be granted restraining the defendants from continuing to employ them.

(h) An employee is under no duty to disclose facts which are inimical to his employer (*Fletcher* v. *Krell* (1872)) though he must not misrepresent the true position.

Bell v. *Lever Bros.* (1932)

Bell was paid £30,000 compensation for loss of office as a director of a firm. Subsequently it was discovered that during his period of office, he had been guilty of certain breaches of his duties which would have entitled his employers to dismiss him without compensation. Bell had not directed his mind to these breaches when he accepted the money.

Held, the compensation agreement was valid.

However, if through his failure to disclose the relevant facts, the employee is injured, his employer may have a partial defence in an action for damages.

Cork v. *Kirby MacLean Ltd.* (1952)

The plaintiff failed to inform his employers that he suffered from epileptic fits, which made it unsafe for him to work above ground. He fell from a working platform, and was injured.

Held, the workman was partially at fault in not disclosing his disability to his employers.

6. Duties of Ex-Employees

A contract of employment may give rise to legal duties which subsist after that contract has been terminated. In addition to any restrictions imposed by a covenant (see above), an ex-employee is under a duty not to disclose unlawfully any confidential information to an unauthorised person, and this is so whether or not there is a contractual term to this effect, for this is an implied term of the contract: *Robb* v. *Green* (1895). However, it would be most impractical to restrain an ex-employee from placing his memory at the services of his new employer, and the proper thing to do in these circumstances is to restrain the ex-employee by a properly drawn up covenant which limits the scope of his activities: *Printers and Finishers* v. *Holloway* (1964).

However, an ex-employee cannot be restrained if he discloses wrongful conduct by his employer, for there is "no confidence as to the disclosure of an iniquity" (*Gortside* v. *Outram* (1856)) so that if an ex-employee knows of facts which ought properly to be disclosed to the appropriate authorities (e.g. police, or press) the former employer cannot restrain such disclosure.

Initial Services, Ltd. v. *Putterill* (1967)

The defendant was employed as a manager by the plaintiffs. After leaving his employment, he gave information to a newspaper concerning the conduct of the plaintiffs' business. The newspaper published an article making certain allegations which were highly detrimental to the plaintiffs, who sued for an injunction and damages.

Held, the disclosures by the former employee were justified in the public interest.

7. Duties of the Employer

(a) To pay the agreed wage or remuneration.

(b) There is no duty to provide work (*Turner* v. *Sawdon* (1901)) except:

(i) if the work is essential to enable the employee to earn his wages:

Turner v. *Goldsmith* (1891)

The plaintiff was employed as a commercial traveller, to be paid by commission.

Held, he had to be given a reasonable opportunity to earn his commission.

(ii) if the work is essential to enhance the reputation of the employee.

Clayton and Waller v. *Oliver* (1930)

The respondent was engaged to play a leading role in a musical production. He was subsequently offered a part which was of a lesser nature, which he refused to accept.

Held, he was entitled to damages for the loss of publicity which he had suffered.

(c) To indemnify his employee in respect of all lawful and reasonable expenses incurred: *Gregory* v. *Ford* (1951).

(d) There is no duty on an employer to provide a reference for an employee who wishes to leave. However, if a reference is given which is allegedly defamatory of the employee, the employer may plead:

(i) justification (i.e. that the statement made was true);
(ii) qualified privilege (i.e. that he had a duty to make the statement and the prospective or future employer had an interest in receiving it). Malice, in the sense of spite or ill-will, will destroy this defence.

An employer who gives a reference which he knows to be false may be liable in deceit to a future employer if the latter suffers damage as a result. A reference given negligently may equally have the same result: *Hedley Byrne* v. *Heller* (1961).

(e) An employer is under a three-fold duty at *common law* to provide for the safety of his employees (see below).

8. Termination of the Contract of Employment

Either party may lawfully terminate the contract of employment on giving appropriate notice (unless it is for a fixed term). The amount of notice to be given depends on the terms of the contract, and in the absence of such terms, reasonable notice must be given. What is reasonable depends on the circumstances of the case, the position held by the employee, etc.

THE CONTRACTS OF EMPLOYMENT ACT 1963 provides for certain *minimum* periods of notice, which apply irrespective of any agreement to the contrary. If an employee has worked for a period of more than 26 weeks but less than two years, he is entitled to one week's notice; for more than two years but less than five, two weeks' notice; for more than five years, four weeks' notice. Unless there is a term to the contrary, an employee is only bound to give one week's notice, irrespective of his length of service.

SUMMARY DISMISSAL is said to be a strong measure, which is justifiable only in the most exceptional circumstances, e.g. for a serious breach of the duty of faithful service. A strike or wilful misconduct could be a breach of that duty. Disobedience is grounds for summary dismissal if it is of such a nature as to make it impossible for the parties to be restored to their former positions.

Pepper v. *Webb* (1969)

The plaintiff was employed by the defendant as a gardenner. He was told to put in some plants, but he rudely refused, and the employer dismissed him. The plaintiff claimed damages for wrongful dismissal.

Held, as he had wilfully disobeyed a lawful and reasonable order, the action must fail.

However, the test to apply is the standards of men, not angels! A single act of insubordination in the heat of the moment is unlikely to be grounds for dismissal.

Laws v. *News Chronicle* (1959)

The plaintiff was employed by the defendant company. Her immediate superior had an argument with the managing director and walked out of the room. The plaintiff followed him out, despite the fact that the managing director told her to stay. Consequently she was dismissed summarily.

Held, she was entitled to damages for wrongful dismissal.

An employee is entitled to refuse to obey orders which are unlawful or unreasonable. Drunkenness, if persistent, may be grounds for dismissal, though hardly a single festive act. Other grounds exist, such as immorality, etc., but these may depend on the nature of the business and the position of the employee. Negligence or incompetence may justify dismissal, though it is a question of fact and degree in each case: *Gould* v. *Webb* (1855). The nature of the negligent act may be of greater relevance than its consequences: *Savage* v. *British India Steam Navigation Co.* (1930). To borrow the employer's money or property without authorisation, even though it is intended to return it, may equally justify instant dismissal: *Sinclair* v. *Neighbour* (1966).

9. Wages and Other Terms

(a) WAGES are the consideration for the contract, and are frequently fixed by negotiation between the parties. They can also be fixed by the terms of a collective agreement made between the employer (or employers' federation) and a trade union. The rates laid down in such agreements will become part of a contract of employment if:

 (i) there is an incorporation of the terms of the collective agreement into the individual contract of employment by express reference (*National Coal Board* v. *Galley* (1958)) or by a notice given under the Contracts of Employment Act 1963: *Camden Exhibition & Display, Ltd.* v. *Lynott* (1965);

 (ii) there is an implied incorporation: *MacLea* v. *Essex Lines* (1932);

 (iii) under the *Terms and Conditions of Employment Act* 1959, s. 8, a complaint to the Industrial Court that the employer is paying wages which are less than those generally recognised may result in an Order that those terms be incorporated as implied terms into the individual contracts of employment (see below).

Certain Acts of Parliament lay down minimum wages to be paid in specified industries, e.g. Wages Councils Act 1959.

UNDER THE FAIR WAGES CLAUSE, any employer who wishes to obtain Government contracts must show that he has observed the recognised terms and conditions laid down for the industry by recognised machinery (see below). Similar provisions are to be found in a large number of statutes giving grants, loans, subsidies, etc., and local authorities frequently insert a similar clause in their contracts.

(b) PROTECTION OF WAGES—It is an offence to pay wages in anything other than current coin of the realm: (Truck Act 1831) but this provision only applies to "workmen" as defined in the Employer and Workman Act 1875 which, generally speaking, means manual workers.

Nonetheless, certain deductions are permissible, including;

(i) deductions for medical attention and medicine, and certain tools. Such deductions must not exceed the real and true value of the items in question, and must be authorised by a written agreement signed by the workman: Truck Act 1831.

(ii) Certain statutory provisions enable employers to make the necessary deductions for income tax, national insurance, national superannuation, etc.

(iii) A payment by the employer to a third party at the request of the employee (e.g. the payment of union dues) does not contravene the Act: *Hewlett v. Allen* (1894).

The Payment by Wages Act 1960 makes provision for the payment of wages by cheque or by postal order where the employer receives a written request from the employee. A written statement must be given with full details of the gross wage, and the amount of lawful deductions. Payment in like manner can be made if the employee is ill or absent because of his work.

(c) BONUSES may be legally payable in certain circumstances, depending on the contractual provisions. In *Powell* v. *Braun* (1954) a reasonable sum was awarded by the Court in lieu of a promised (but unspecified) bonus, but in *Grieve* v. *Imperial Tobacco* (1963) it was held that the bonus was a mere gratuitous payment, and conferred no automatic right on the employee to receive it.

(d) WAGES DURING SICKNESS can be claimed by the employee if there is no agreement to the contrary (*Orman* v. *Saville Sportswear* (1960)) but there may be an implied term of the contract which negates this: (*O'Grady* v. *Saper* (1940)).

(d) HOLIDAYS WITH PAY will depend on express or implied agreement, the express or implied incorporation of the terms of a collective agreement and (possibly) the customs of the trade or industry. *The Holidays with Pay Act* 1938 enables a wage regulating body (e.g. a Wages Council) to specify the holidays with pay in respect of employees covered by statutory minimum wage rates.

(f) HOURS OF WORK and overtime are fixed by the parties by agreement, or by the terms of the collective agreement (above). Certain statutory maxima exist, e.g. in coal mining. Women and young persons have their hours of work limited by the *Factories Act* 1961, s. 86. *post*, page 42.

10. Disciplinary powers of the Employer

(a) FINES FOR MISCONDUCT—These are permissible providing the terms of the Truck Act 1896 are strictly adhered to. The fine must be provided for in a written contract or prominently displayed notice; it may be imposed only for acts which cause loss or damage to the business; the offence for which the fines can be made must be clearly specified; the fine must be fair and reasonable, and written particulars must be given to the employee.

(b) DEDUCTIONS FOR NEGLIGENT WORK, as for fines, above. The deduction must not exceed the actual loss or estimated value for which the employee is responsible.

(c) SUSPENSION—This is only permitted if there is a term to this effect in the contract of employment, either expressly, or through the incorporation of the terms of a collective agreement. A suspension is not illegal by virtue of the Truck Acts, for it is not a deduction or fine, but part of the contractual obligations incurred: *Bird* v. *British Celanese* (1945). An employee wrongly suspended may recover his lost wages by way of damages: (*Hanley* v. *Pease* (1915)) but he is under a duty to mitigate his loss.

(d) DISCIPLINARY PROCEDURES—These are frequently found in the collective agreement, and may be incorporated into the contract of employment: *Tomlinson* v. *L.M.S. Railway* (1944). Where necessary the rules of natural justice must be observed: *Ridge* v. *Baldwin* (1963).

11. Redundancy Payments

(a) All employed persons may qualify for a payment under the *Redundancy Payment Act* 1965, subject to a number of exceptions, including:

    (i) self-employed persons;
    (ii) employees with less than two years' service;
    (iii) employees who work less than 21 hours per week;

    (iv) employees whose notice expires on retirement age (65 for
        men, 60 for women);
    (v) husbands or wives of employers;
    (vi) Crown Servants and National Health Service employees,
    (vii) registered dock workers;
 (viii) shore fishermen;
    (ix) employees who normally work abroad;
    (x) domestic servants who are close relatives of the employer;
    (xi) employees on a fixed term contract made before the Act
        of at least 2 years duration.

(b) An employee may only claim if he is dismissed *for reason of redundancy*. If a dismissal takes place, it is presumed to be for reason of redundancy, and it is for the employer to show to the contrary.

(c) There is no dismissal if the employer (or his successors) offers to renew the contract or re-engage the employee in suitable alternative employment: *Lloyd* v. *Brassey* (1969). A demotion, or unreasonable transfer, or serious change in the nature of the employment may not be suitable alternative employment.

(d) A notice of possible redundancies in the future is not a dismissal for redundancy, and an employee who leaves on his own to get another job before he is dismissed cannot claim.

(e) A dismissal is for redundancy if the employer has ceased or is about to cease to carry on business, either altogether, or in the place where the employee is working: *McCulloch* v. *Moore* (1968). It is also a redundancy situation if the need for employees to do a particular type of work, or do such work in a particular place, has diminished or ceased. The test is, have the basic requirements of the business changed? Thus a new method of doing the work may lead to redundancies, but a reorganisation which imposes higher or more onerous duties on the employee is not redundancy: *North Riding Garages* v. *Butterwick* (1967).

(f) A useful, but not conclusive, method of ascertaining whether redundancy exists is to ask, was the employee replaced? If he was not, it is probable though not certain, that he was redundant.

(g) An employee who is dismissed because of misconduct or disobedience is not redundant, unless he disobeyed an order to do another kind of work because his own work was diminishing, and his refusal was justified, in which case he is redundant.

(h) An offer to re-engage, if different from the old contract, must be in writing. If such an offer is reasonable, and is refused, no payment can be claimed. What is reasonable alternative employment is a question of fact, to be determined by such considerations as the nature of the business, the effect of the new employment on the employee's domestic life, travelling time, remuneration, availability of accommodation, the nature of the new work in relation to the old, loss of fringe benefits, such as overtime, and all other relevant factors.

A claim under the Act may lie if there has been short-time working or a lay-off lasting for more than four weeks, or six weeks out of 13 consecutive weeks. (But not if this was caused by an industrial dispute). The employee must notify his employer *in writing* his intention to claim, and give notice to quit his employment. The employer may then serve a counter-notice stating that he intends to resume normal workings within four weeks for a period of not less than three months.

(j) Payment is based on (1) age and (2) length of service. At the moment, for men it is worked out as follows:

   (i) for every year of service between 18 and 21 . . . . . $\frac{1}{2}$ week's pay;

   (ii) for every year of service between 22 and 40...1 week's pay;

   (iii) for every year of service between 41 and 64 . . . . 1$\frac{1}{2}$ weeks' pay;

   (iv) for every month between 64 and 65, reduce payment by 1/12th;

   (v) earnings in excess of £40 are to be disregarded;

   (vi) maximum number of years to be counted is 20.

(k) Disputes are referred to the Industrial Tribunal from which an appeal lies to the High Court. Normally, each side will pay its own costs before the Tribunal, but there is a discretion to award costs up to £25 in the event of an application being frivolous, etc.

12. Employer's Common Law Duty to Provide for the Safety of his Employees—The employer must:

(a) supply and maintain safe plant and appliances, proper for the work for which they are required or to be used;

(b) ensure a safe system of working;

(c) engage reasonable competent fellow employees.

GENERAL

(i) These duties are personal to the employer, and he cannot absolve himself from liability be delegating this responsibility to someone else: *Wilson and Clyde Co.* v. *English* (1938). There is a duty not to expose employees to unnecessary risks, and this extends to matters which are ancillary to the employer's business, as well as those matters which arise from the ordinary course of business.

Sumner v. *William Henderson* (1964)

The defendants engaged contractors to lay new electrical wiring in their store. A fire broke out, and an employee was killed.

Held, the employers were liable.

(ii) If an employer purchases tools or equipment from a reputable supplier, he has performed his duty, not delegated it; *Davie* v. *New Merton Board Mills* (1959). However, the Employers' Liability (Defective Equipment) Act 1969 provides that if an employee suffers personal injury in consequence of a defect in equipment provided by his employer, and the defect is attributable to the fault of a third party (e.g., the supplier), the injury shall be deemed to be attributable to the negligence of the employer.

(iii) The duty to take care does not extend to the property of the employee, e.g. clothing, etc.: *Edwards* v. *West Hertfordshire Hospital Management Committee* (1957).

(iv) The duty at *common law* is not an absolute duty (as are many of the duties imposed by the Factories Act or other statutes). The duty is only to take *reasonable care*. Thus if an employer can show that he acted in a careful and prudent manner, he will not be liable (see below).

A. SAFE PLANT AND APPLIANCES

(i) An employer must provide safe plant, tools, equipment etc., which are suitable for the work to be done in the conditions prevalent at the time.

Bradford v. *Robinson Rentals* (1967)

The plaintiff was employed as a van driver by the defendants.

He was ordered to drive some 500 miles in an exceptionally cold spell of weather, and, because the van was unheated, suffered frost-bite.

Held, the employers were liable for negligence in exposing him to a forseeable risk.

If the tools or materials are inherently dangerous, the employer must take steps to minimise those dangers by taking adequate precautions.

Naismith v. *London Film Productions* (1939)

An actress was required to wear inflammable materials for filming purposes. These ignited, causing serious burns.

Held, the employers would be liable unless they could show they had taken all reasonable precautions to make the work safe.

(ii) The duty extends to all those acts by the employee which are reasonably necessary and incidental to the work to be done.

Davidson v. *Handley Page* (1945)

The plaintiff, while washing a tea-cup for her own use, slipped on a duck-board, due to the greasy condition of the floor.

Held, her employers were liable.

(iii) The employer is not liable for the safety of his employees who are working on someone else's premises, and over which he has no control, though the occupier of those premises may be liable under the Occupier's Liability Act 1957. However, the employer may be liable if he fails to minimise these dangers by not ensuring a safe system of working on those premises.

General Cleaning Co. v. *Christmas* (1953)

A company contracted to clean the windows of an office block. A window cleaner fell while standing outside a window.

Held, his employers were liable for failing to so organise the work as to prevent an employee from falling.

(iv) If an employer knows, or ought to know, that a machine or tool is dangerous (e.g. it has a tendency to break or eject parts) then he must take steps to safeguard his employee. *Close* v. *Steel Co. of Wales* (1961), *post per* LORD GODDARD. Unsuitable tools or equipment should be withdrawn from circulation by the employer.

Taylor v. *Rover Co., Ltd.* (1966)

An employee was injured when a piece of steel from a chisel flew into his eye. There had previously been a similar accident, but the employers had not withdrawn the tools from circulation.

Held, the employers were liable.

B. SAFE SYSTEM OF WORKING

(i) What is a safe system depends on all the circumstances of each case; the work, the layout, the provision of warnings, safety precautions, protective clothing, special instruction, training, etc. are all factors which must be taken into consideration. An employer will be liable if he fails to devise a safe method of doing the work, or permits an unsafe method to continue.

Barcock v. *Brighton Corporation* (1949)

The defendant was employed at an electricity sub-station. A certain method of testing was in operation, which was contrary to the regulations and unsafe, but this was unknown to him. He was subsequently injured while carrying out a test.

Held, the employers were liable, as they had failed to devise a safe system.

(ii) If safety devices are to be used, they must be available at the place where they are needed.

Finch v. *Telegraph Construction and Maintenance Co.* (1949)

The plaintiff was employed as a grinder. Goggles were made available by the employers, but he had not been told where he could find them. He was injured by a flying fragment of metal.

Held, the employers were liable.

But if an employer can show that even if he provided safety equipment, they would not have been used, he will not be liable

for an accident which occurs, for his negligence was not the cause
of the injury.

MacWilliams v. *Sir William Arroll & Co.* (1962)

An experienced steel erector fell during his work and was
killed. The employers had, in the past, provided safety belts,
but the employees had never used them, so they were taken
away to another site.

Held, even if the safety belts had been available, it was
probable that the deceased would not have worn one;
consequently, although the employers were negligent, the
negligence was not the cause of the death.

Further, if safety precautions are provided, and the employee
is properly instructed on how to use them, it is not the duty of
the employer to stand over the men and see that those precautions
are carried out.

Woods v. *Durable Suites* (1953)

The plaintiff contracted dermatitis after using a synthetic
glue. A barrier cream was available, but the employer did not
compel its use.

Held, the employer had fulfilled his common law duty by
providing the safety precautions.

An employer has fulfilled his duty if he provides safety equipment,
informs his employees, and leaves it to them to decide whether
or not to use them.

James v. *Hepworth & Grandage, Ltd.* (1967)

The employer provided spats, gloves and aprons to protect
their employees from the dangers of molten metal, and also
put up large notices informing employees that these were
available, and that they should be used for protection. In
fact, few employees wore spats. The plaintiff was injured
by molten metal, which would not have happened if he had
worn spats.

Held, the employers had fulfilled their duty by providing
spats, informing the employees of their availability, and letting
them choose whether to wear them or not.

(iii) If, because of the physical peculiarities of an employee, a risk of greater injury exists with respect to that employee, a higher duty of care exists to ensure that no accident will befall him.

Paris v. *Stepney Borough Council* (1951)

The appellant, who had only one eye, was employed by the respondents. He was totally blinded when a chip of metal flew into his good eye. It was not the practice of employers to provide goggles to men employed on his kind of work.

Held, the gravity of the consequences if an accident should occur was a relevant factor in determining whether or not the employer had taken reasonable care for the employee's safety. In the circumstances, the employers should have provided protective eye-shields.

C. REASONABLY COMPETENT FELLOW EMPLOYEES

An employer will be liable if an employee is injured through the negligence or lack of skill of a fellow employee, for the employer should only take on competent staff.

Olsen v. *Corry and Gravesend Aviation Co.* (1936)

The defendants' manager taught a trainee an unsafe method of working, with the result that the latter was injured.

Held, the employers were liable.

An employer will also be liable if he continues to employ a workman whom he knows has a habit of "skylarking," and whose activities injure a fellow employee: *Hudson* v. *Ridge Manufacturing Co.* (1957); but this does not apply if one workman plays a practical joke on another which results in an injury, provided the act was not done in the scope of the employment, and the employer had no reason to expect that such a prank would be played: *Coddington* v. *National Harvester Co.* (1969).

D. DEFENCE TO AN ACTION BASED ON COMMON LAW NEGLIGENCE

(i) The employer may always claim that he was not negligent, i.e. that he did all that a reasonable employer would have done in the circumstances.

Latimer v. *A.E.C.* (1953)

Due to a heavy rainfall, water flooded a factory leaving the
floor in a slippery state. The employers spread sand and
sawdust when the water subsided, but there was not enough
to treat the whole factory. The plaintiff slipped on a greasy
part, and was injured.

Held, the employers had done all they could in the circumstances. It would have been unreasonable to close the
whole factory because of a remote chance of injury.

(ii) The Law Reform (Contributory Negligence) Act 1945
provides that if a person suffers damage, partly as a result of his
own fault, and partly because of the fault of another, damages may
be reduced to the extent the court thinks fit, having regard to the
claimant's share in the responsibility for the damage. Thus in
a large number of cases, damages are in practice reduced by a
percentage, depending on the extent to which the court considers
that the employee was himself responsible for the injury due to
his own failure to take care.

(iii) *Volenti non fit injuria.* "To him that is willing, no legal
harm is done." A person who consents to the risk of being
injured cannot be heard to complain about it. However, this
defence rarely succeeds in employment cases, for the courts
refuse to equate knowledge of the risk with consent to run the
risk: *Smith* v. *Baker* (1891). Merely because an employee knows
of a danger, it does not follow that he consents to run the risk of
being injured.

Bowater v. *Rowley Regis Corporation* (1944)

The plaintiff was ordered to take out a horse. He protested,
because he knew that the horse had been restive on other
occasions, but eventually agreed to carry out the order.
The horse subsequently bolted, and he was injured.

Held, it was not part of his employment to manage unruly
horses, and he had not voluntarily accepted the risk.

It must be shown that the consent was to the risk of being injured
without compensation, e.g. stunt artistes. However, if there is a
safe and an unsafe method of doing the work, and the employees
choose the unsafe method, the employer may escape liability.

Imperial Chemical Industries v. *Shatwell* (1964)

Two experienced shotfirers knew that they should not proceed with their work unless all persons in the vicinity had withdrawn to safety. In breach of all instructions, they carried out a test in the open, and were injured by the resultant explosion.

Held, the employers were not liable.

13. Liability of the Employer for his Employees' Actions Which Cause Injury or Damage to Third Parties

(a) The employee is always personally liable for his own wrongful actions. In addition, however, an employer may be vicariously liable for such acts which are committed in the scope of the employee's employment.

(b) The employer will be liable in two sets of circumstances:
    (i) if he authorises or ratifies the employee's actions or
    (ii) if the employee was doing an act which was authorised by the employer, but in a mode or manner which was not authorised. In other words, the employer will be liable for the way in which the employee does his work.

Bayley v. *Manchester and Sheffield Rail Co.* (1873)

A railway porter pulled a passenger out of a railway carriage in the belief that he was on the wrong train.

Held, the porter was doing what he was employed to do, i.e. see that passengers arrived at the right destination. His manner of doing the work was unauthorised, but the employers were liable for an injury sustained by the plaintiff.

(c) If the employer prohibits the employee from doing a certain act, this will limit the scope of the employment.

Twine v. *Bean's Express* (1946)

The defendants expressly prohibited drivers from giving lifts to unauthorised persons, and fixed a notice to this effect in the driver's cab. A driver gave a lift to a hitch-hiker, who was killed because of the driver's negligence.

Held, the driver had no authority to give lifts, and the employers were not liable.

C

If the employer prohibits the employee from doing his work in a certain manner, a wrongful act contrary to those instructions may still be within the scope of employment.

Limpus v. *London General Omnibus Co.* (1862)

The defendant company had expressly forbidden their drivers to race with other buses. In breach of these instructions, one of their drivers took a corner at high speed, and injured the plaintiff.

Held, the company were liable. The employee was doing what he was employed to do, even though the manner in which he did it was unauthorised and forbidden.

(d) An act done to protect the employer's property is within the scope of employment (*Poland* v. *Parr* (1927)) but excessive zeal may take the wrongful act outside the scope of the employment.

Warren v. *Henleys, Ltd.* (1948)

A petrol pump attendant assaulted the plaintiff after a quarrel about payment.

Held, the employee was acting outside the course of his employment because he was pursuing a personal grudge.

(e) The scope of an employee's employment extends to all acts which are incidental to that employment but not to acts which are permitted or tolerated, but which are not part of the employee's duties.

Century Insurance Co. v. *Northern Ireland Road Transport Board* (1942)

A lorry driver employed by the respondents was delivering petrol to a garage. He lit a cigarette and threw away the match. An explosion, causing considerable damage, resulted.

Held, the employers were liable for the negligent manner in which the employee did his work.

Crook v. *Derbyshire Stone, Ltd.* (1956)

A lorry driver employed by the defendants was permitted to break his journey in order to have refreshments. He stopped his lorry opposite a cafe, and while crossing the road, collided with the plaintiff, who was injured.

Held, having refreshments was no part of the employee's duties, and the employer was not liable.

(f) An employer will not be liable if the employee is on a frolic of his own, or is using the employer's time or property for his own purposes: *Storey* v. *Ashton* (1869).

14. Employer's Liability for the Wrongful Acts of his Independent Contractors

(a) Generally speaking, the employer is not liable for such acts (*Sharpe* v. *Sweeting* (1963)) though he may be if he failed to select the contractor with care and reasonable diligence.

(b) Exceptionally, however, he will be liable:

- (i) If the employer is under a statutory duty to do a task, or to do it in a certain way, he cannot absolve himself from responsibility by employing an independent contractor: *Hole* v. *Sittingbourne Railway* (1861).
- (ii) If an employer instructs the contractor to do work which is unlawful, he will be responsible for those acts: *Ellis* v. *Sheffild Gas Consumers Co.* (1853).
- (iii) If the work is of a dangerous nature, the employer must ensure that adequate safety precautions are taken: *Holiday* v. *National Telephone Co.* (1899).
- (iv) If the employer personally interferes with the work of the contractor, or gives negligent instructions: *Burgess* v. *Gray* (1845).
- (v) If the employer engages more than one sub-contractor to do certain work, or if he exercises some form of control over the co-ordination of the work, he may be under a duty to ensure that the work can be carried out in safety, and thus be liable for any injuries suffered by an employee of the sub-contractor which he could have foreseen: *McArdle* v. *Andmac Roofing Co.* (1967).

15. Employer's Personal Liability for Criminal Acts Committed by his Employees in the course of the Employment

Generally speaking, an employer is not liable for these, unless he orders the commission of the act or failed to restrain it when he knew it was criminal: *Parkinson* v. *Levinson* (1951). He will be criminally liable if:

(a) The act amounts to a public nuisance, and this is so even though the act was contrary to instructions, done without the employer's knowledge, or was a departure from the normal method of working.

(b) A number of Acts of Parliament create statutory offences, for which the employer will be liable even though he is unaware of their commission: *Bond* v. *Evans* (1888). Generally this depends on:

    (i) The wording of the Act;
   (ii) the objects of Parliament;
  (iii) the nature of the duty;
  (iv) the person upon whom the duty is imposed;
   (v) the person who would normally perform the act;
  (vi) the person to be punished: *Mousell Bros.* v. *London and North Western Railway* (1917).

(c) Many statutes provide a defence for the employer if he can show that he was not aware of the offence and was not lacking in care in failing to prevent or discover it.

16. Employer's Liability to Third Persons for the Criminal Acts of his Employees

If the act is within the scope of the employee's employment, an employer will be liable to a third party who is injured or suffers damage, even though the employee's actions amount to a criminal offence.

Morris v. *Martin* (1965)

The plaintiff sent her mink stole to a furrier for cleaning, who sent it to the defendants. An employee of the defendants stole it.

Held, the defendants were liable to the plaintiff for the criminal act of their employee.

Chapter 2 *Industrial Legistlation*

Britain has a comprehensive system of legislation designed to ensure the health, safety and welfare of employed persons. The two most important Acts are (i) the Factories Act 1961, which covers about 11 million persons, and (ii) the Offices, Shops and Railway Premises Act 1963, which covers about 8 million employees. Other legislation extends protection to a further 3 million persons. Liability under these various Acts is generally irrespective of the breach of any common law rule.

1. The Factories Act 1961

1. The Act applies to all factories within the statutory definition, which is (section 175): "Any premises in which, or within the close or curtilage or precincts of which, persons are employed in manual labour in any process for or incidental to any of the following purposes, namely:—

(a) the making of any article or part of any article; or

(b) the altering, repairing, ornamenting, finishing, cleaning, or washing or the breaking up or demolition of any article; or

(c) the adapting for sale of any article: or

(d) the slaughtering of cattle; or

(e) the confinement of such animals while awaiting slaughter; being premises in which, or within the close or curtilage or precincts of which, the work is carried on by way of trade or for purposes of gain and to or over which the employer of the persons employed therein has the right to access or control."

2. The definition includes the following additional premises in which persons are employed in manual labour, namely, dry docks, premises where articles are sorted out as a preliminary to work in the factory, premises where bottles or containers are filled or washed or articles are packed, premises where yarn or cloth is made up or packed, printing or bookbinding works, locomotive building and repair shops, film sets, premises where film or theatrical dresses or properties are made, any laundry incidental to a business or public institution, premises where articles are made or prepared incidental to the carrying on of building operations or works of engineering construction, etc.

3. The following points must be noted about the definition;

(a) There must be manual labour employed or used, but this does not imply strenuous exertion.

Hoare v. *Green* (1907)

A room behind a florist's shop, wherein persons were employed to make wreaths, bouquets, etc. was held to be a factory.

The fact that a person is employed in manual labour carrying boxes or crates does not make the premises a factory (*Joyce* v. *Boots Cash Chemists* (1950), but one person may be employed in a factory if it is otherwise within the statutory definition.

Haygarth v. *Stone Lighting and Radio Co.* (1966)

An engineer was employed to repair radio and television sets in a room at the rear of a shop where such sets were being sold.

Held, the room was a factory.

(b) A wide meaning is given to the word "article," and it includes water, gas and electricity.

Longhurst v. *Guildford, Godalming & District Water Board* (1961)

A pumping station, where water was put under pressure for distribution was held not to be a factory. However, had the accident occurred in the filtering station, the defendant would have been liable.

(c) "Adapting for sale" means that it should be a little different than it was before.

Grove v. *Lloyd's British Testing Co.* (1931)

Cables and anchors were being tested in a building to see if they were fit for sale.
Held, the premises were not a factory.

(d) The Act applies to the Crown and to Municipal Authorities, even though they may not carry on the work by way of trade, or for purposes of gain (section 175 (9)), but this does not extend the definition of the Act to include the workshops of a technical college (*Weston* v. *London County Council* (1941)), the kitchen of a hospital (*Wood* v. *London County Council* (1941)) or a prison workshop (*Pullen* v. *Prison Commissioners* (1957)) for these do not engage in trade or operate for purposes of gain.

(e) Since the Act provides that the employer must have the right of access and control it follows that outworkers are not within its scope.

(f) If premises are within the curtilage of a factory, but are used for some purpose other than the processes carried on in the factory, those premises shall not be deemed to be a factory unless they would otherwise be within the definition. Thus a building within the curtilage of a factory which contains a restaurant for managerial and administrative staff was not regarded as being incidental to the purposes of the factory (*Thomas* v. *British Thomson-Heuston* (1953)), though a workers' canteen was so regarded: *Luttman* v. *I.C.I.* (1955). But a building which has a separate purpose to the factory may, if it is otherwise within the definition, still be a factory.

Newton v. *John Stanning* (1962)

A pump house within the curtilage of a textile factory, which was used to pump water inside the factory was held to be within the statutory definition.

Thurogood v. *Van den Burghs and Jurgens* (1951)

Within the curtilage of a factory was a building where

maintenance work was carried out on machinery which was being used in the factory. The plaintiff was injured while testing an electric fan which was in for repair.

Held, the premises were a factory, and he was entitled to recover damages.

4. PART I GENERAL HEALTH PROVISIONS

The requirements are as follows:—

Section 1. Every factory must be kept clean, regularly cleaned, washed, painted and whitewashed.

Section 2. A factory shall not be so overcrowded so as to cause risk of injury to the health of employees. The number employed in any workroom shall not be such that it works out less than 400 cubic feet per person.

Section 3. A reasonable temperature shall be maintained, and if a substantial proporton of the work is done sitting, and does not involve serious physical effort, a temperature of less than 60 degrees after the first hour will be unreasonable.

Section 4. Adequate ventilation shall be provided, and fumes, dust and other impurities caused in the process shall be rendered harmless.

Section 5. Suitable and sufficient lighting, whether natural or artificial, shall be provided in every part of the factory in which persons are working or passing. If there is adequate lighting but the employers do not turn it on they are in breach of this section: (*Thornton* v. *Fisher & Ludlow, Ltd.* (1968)). Under sub-section (2), the Minister has the power to make regulations prescribing a standard of sufficient and suitable lighting: *Lane* v. *Gloucester Engineering Co.* (1967).

Section 6. Deals with the drainage of floors where any process is likely to render the floor wet to an appreciable extent.

Section 7. Requires sufficient and suitable sanitary conveniences to be provided for both sexes, be maintained and kept clean.

Section 11. Empowers the Minister to make special regulations requiring medical supervision in certain circumstances.

5. PART II   GENERAL SAFETY PROVISIONS

Section 12. Requires that prime movers (i.e. machinery which provides mechanical energy) shall be securely fenced. Every part of electric generators, motors and rotary converters shall be securely fenced unless it is in such a position or of such construction as to be as safe to every person employed or working on the premises as it would be if securely fenced.

Section 13. Every part of the transmission machinery (i.e. machinery by which the motion of a prime mover is transmitted to the machine) shall be securely fenced unless it is in such a position or of such construction as to be as safe to every person employed or working on the premises as it would be if securely fenced.

Section 14. Every dangerous part of any machinery shall be securely fenced unless it is in such a position or of such construction as to be as safe to any person employed or working on the premises as it would be if securely fenced. By sub-section (2), this requirement is satisfied if the machine is fitted with a device which automatically prevents the operator from coming into contact with the machine. By sub-section (6) The Minister may make special regulations in relation to the fencing of materials or articles which are dangerous while in motion in the machine. It should be noted that the Minister may also, by virtue of section 76, make regulations modifying the provisions of Parts I, II and IV of the Act, and such regulations will supercede the provisions of the Act: *Miller* v. *William Boothman* (1944).

The following points should be noted arising from these sections:

(a) What is meant by "machinery"? No definition of this word is given in the Act, and the ordinary meaning of the word is to be given. The Act says "machinery", not "machine." An overhead cable way was held not to be machinery (*Quintas* v. *National Smelting Co.* (1961)) and while a mobile fork-lift truck was similarly regarded (*Cherry* v. *International Alloys* (1960)) this case was specifically overruled: *British Railways Board* v. *Liprot* (1967). The test seems to be whether or not the machinery in question is part of the factory equipment, and if it is, it is irrelevant whether it is static or mobile.

British Railways Board v. *Liprot* (1967)

A mobile crane, which was mounted on a four-wheeled chassis with rubber wheels, was capable of moving under its

own power. The respondent was injured when he was caught
between the revolving body of the crane and the wheels.

Held, the employers were liable for their failure to fence a
dangerous part of machinery.

(b) When is a part of machinery dangerous? The oft-cited
answer is "A part of machinery is dangerous if it is a possible
cause of injury to anybody acting in a way in which a human
being may reasonably be expected to act in circumstances which
may be reasonably be expected to occur": *per* Du Parcq, J. in
Walker v. *Bletchley Flettons* (1937).

The following acts have been held to be forseeable, and thus give
rise to an obligation to fence a dangerous part of machinery.

(i) Carelessness

Smith v. *Chesterfield Co-operative Society* (1953)

The plaintiff worked on a machine, the rollers of which
were protected by a guard to within three inches of the bed
of the machine. Despite instructions to the contrary, she
placed her fingers under the guard, and was injured.

Held, her conduct was forseeable.

(ii) Indolence, weariness and disobedience.

Woodley v. *Meason Freer* (1963)

Employees were warned not to put their hands in a machine
in order to remove obstructions. A workman acted contrary
to this instruction, and was injured.

Held, the employers were guilty of an offence in failing to
fence the machine.

(iii) Stupidity

Uddin v. *Associated Portland Cement* (1965)

The plaintiff climbed a ladder in an attempt to catch a pigeon
which had flown into the factory. He caught his clothing on
a dangerous part of machinery which was not fenced.

Held, the employers were liable. The Act is designed to
protect persons who are "employed *or* working on the
premises," and the fact that the plaintiff committed an act of
folly was only relevant in assessing his contributory negligence.

On the other hand, the following acts have been held to be not forseeable.

(i) Craziness.

Rushton v. *Turner Asbestos* (1959)

An employee was told not to put his hand into a machine. He did so, and was injured.

Held, although the employers were in breach of their statutory obligations under section 14, for which they may well be liable for criminal penalties (see *Woodley* v. *Meason Freer, supra*), they were not liable in a civil action for damages. The workman's own negligence was the sole cause of the accident.

(ii) Pervesity.

Carr v. *Mercantile Products* (1949)

The plaintiff, working on a machine, forced her hand into a hole three inches in diameter.

Held, she was the authoress of her own misfortune.

It follows that if the injury could not be reasonably forseen, the employer will not be liable.

Burns v. *Joseph Terry* (1950)

The plaintiff climbed a ladder to get some objects on a shelf. The ladder slipped, and he caught his hand on an unguarded part of the machine.

Held, the employers were not liable. The machine was guarded against such dangers as were reasonably forseeable.

However, forseeability is relevant to the conduct of the employee, not the operation of the machine. Thus if a worker is injured on an unfenced part of dangerous machinery, and the injury would not have occured if the part had been securely fenced, the employer will be liable even though the accident occured in an entirely unforseeable manner: *Millard* v. *Serck Tubes* (1969).

If the machine is doing work it was designed to do, a part of that machine may be dangerous through the juxtaposition of that part and pieces of materials being used on the machine: *Midlands and Low Moor Iron and Steel Co.* v. *Cross* (1964)). But there is no duty to fence against the juxtaposition of one piece of machinery *and another machine,* or a danger caused by the proximity of a moving part of a machine and some other stationary extraneous object.

Pearce v. *Stanley-Bridges* (1965)

The plaintiff was injured when his arm was caught between the rising platform of a lifting machine and a conveyor belt.

Held, the Act did not impose an obligation to fence a "gap" between two machines. Moreover, the alleged danger was not reasonably forseeable, and for both these reasons the claim must fail.

If a dangerous part of machinery is not securely fenced, and an employee is injured with no evidence to show how that injury occurred, the employers will still be liable for a breach of their statutory duty, for there is a presumption that the accident would not have happened had the employers not been in breach of their statutory duties.

Allen v. *Aeroplane & Motor Aluminium Castings* (1965)

The plaintiff was injured on a machine which was not fenced. The trial judge did not believe his account of the incident, and gave judgment for the employers.

Held, there must be judgment for the plaintiff notwithstanding that he had not given an acceptable account of the accident.

(c) When is a dangerous part of machinery securely fenced? It must be remembered that the duty is to fence, not to provide a substitute for fencing.

Chasterney v. *Nairn* (1937)

The employers put up a notice which read "Do not put your hands in the machinery while it is in motion. Persons disregard this notice at their own risk."

Held, the provisions of the Act had not been complied with, and the employers were guilty of an offence.

Since the duty is an absolute one, the Act thus prohibits the use of machinery which cannot be operated with a fence.

Summers (John) & Sons, Ltd. v. Frost (1955)

A workman injured his thumb while using a grinding stone. To fence the machine would be to make it unusable.

Held, the fact that it was commercially impractical to fence the machine was no defence.

The fence must not merely be a barrier (*Quintas* v. *National Smelting Co.* (1960) *per* DEVLIN, J.) but sufficient to protect a worker adequately. A fence does not cease to be secure merely because its protection can be circumvented and rendered useless by some act of perverse and deliberate ingenuity: *Carr* v. *Mercantile Products* (1949) (*supra*). The purpose of the fence is to prevent the worker from coming into contact with the machine, not to protect the worker from being injured by parts of the machine which may fly out.

Close v. Steel Co. of Wales (1961)

The bit of a portable electric drill shattered and injured the appellant in his eye. Such shatterings were common, but a serious accident had never occurred before.

Held, the employers were under no duty to fence.

Nor need the fence protect against flying particles of materials used by the machine (*Nicholls* v. *Austin* (1946)) though in appropriate circumstances such accidents may give rise to an action for common law negligence: *Close* v. *Steel Co. of Wales,* (1962) *per* LORD GODDARD. If a machine makes an "uncovenanted stroke" (i.e. one it was not designed to do), this is not forseeable: *Eaves* v. *Morris Motors* (1961). Nor does the Act protect a worker if he is injured because a tool he is using is caught on a dangerous part (*Sparrow* v. *Fairey Aviation* (1961)) though the Act does apply if his clothing is caught, causing him injury.

Lovelidge v. Anselm Odling (1967)

A tie worn by the plaintiff was caught in a machine and as a result he suffered an injury.

Held, the employers were liable for failing to fence the machine. (Note: the case was decided on the Construction (General Provision) Regulations, the wording of which is the same as the Factories Act. See also *Uddin* v. *Associated Portland Cement, supra*).

The duty to fence extends to machines which are being used in the factory, not to those which are being made (*Parvin* v. *Morton Machine Co.* (1951). There is no obligation to fence a machine while it is being installed, but once erected, it comes within the Act even though it is not yet in use: *Irwin* v. *White, Tomkins and Courage* (1964). The section requires the machinery to be safe for every person working or employed on the premises, and thus the statutory protection applies to workers who are not authorised to use the machine (*Leach* v. *Standard Telephones* (1966)), but not to a worker who is using the machine for his own purpose and in his own time, even though he does so with his employer's permission: *Napieralski* v. *Curtis* (1959).

Volenti non fit injuria and statutory duties

The doctrine of absolute liability which flows from a breach of statutory duties means that if the employer fails to carry out the terms of the statute, he will be liable. An employee cannot "agree" with his employer to ignore those obligations, and to that extent the defence of "volenti non fit injuria" has no application. If, however, an employee takes all possible steps to ensure compliance, but the employee disregards the precautions and disobeys the employer's instructions, the employer will escape liability, because an employee cannot obtain damages because he has put his employer in breach of the statute: *Manwaring* v. *Billington* (1952).

However, the employer must take all reasonable steps to ensure that the employee carries out those precautions, and if he fails to do so, e.g. by not giving adequate instruction or training, the employer cannot then take advantage of the defence that the fault lay with the injured workman; *Boyle* v. *Kodak* (1969).

Section 16 requires that all fences shall be of substantial construction, constantly maintained and kept in position while the parts required to be fenced are in motion or use, except when such parts are exposed for examination for any lubrication or adjustment. A machine is not in motion or use if it is being moved by an inching button for the purposes of cleaning it (*Knight* v. *Leamington Spa Courier* (1961)) and the courts have drawn a distinction between "being moved" by an inching button, and "in motion" at a fast pace, albeit for only a short time: *Stanbrook* v. *Waterlow* (1964). In deciding whether or not machinery is in motion, account is taken of the speed of the movement, its duration, the method and purpose of starting the machine: *Mitchell* v. *Westin* (1965).

Section 28 requires all floors steps stairs passages and gangways to be of sound construction and properly maintained, and shall, as far as is reasonably practicable, be kept free from any obstruction and from any substance likely to cause persons to slip. Thus there is an absolute duty to maintain the structure of the stairs, steps, etc., but this does not apply to some temporary and exceptional state, such as may be caused by flooding: *Latimer* v. *A.E.C.* (1959). The onus is on the occupier of the factory to show that it was not reasonably practicable to make the conditions any safer: *Nimmo* v. *Alexander Cowan* (1967). An obstruction is something which has no right to be where it is.

Pengelley v. *Bell Punch Co.* (1964).

In a factory, reels of paper were stored in racks and on the floor. While trying to take one down, the plaintiff caught his foot in between two reels, and injured himself.

Held, the reels were not an obstruction, for they were properly there. In order to be an obstruction, the article must be something which has no business to be where it was.

It is immaterial that the slippery substance is on the obstacle, rather than the floor.

Dorman Long v. *Bell* (1964))

The respondent slipped on a greasy metal plate, which was an obstruction.

Held, the employers were liable.

Section 29 provides that the means of access to every place at which any person has at any time to work must be as safe as is reasonably practicable, as well as the actual place of work. This section does not apply solely to permanent physical structures, but to temporary features as well (*Callaghan* v. *Kidd* (1944)), though not if such features are exceptional.

Leversley v. *Thos. Firth* (1953)

The plaintiff tripped over a steel bar and was injured.

Held, in view of its transient and exceptional character, the defendants had not failed to maintain a safe means of access to the work. The employer is not liable for every temporary obstruction which may occur through mischance.

The section is for the protection of any person, not just employees of the occupier: *Lavender* v. *Diamantis* (1949). If the occupier fails to provide proper equipment so that the place of work is not safe, he will be liable.

Ross v. *Associated Portland Cement* (1964)

A workman rested a long ladder against some wire netting, and climbed up it. The netting collapsed, and he fell, sustaining fatal injuries.

Held, the employers, by not providing proper equipment, had failed to keep safe the deceased's place of work, and were therefore liable.

6. OTHER IMPORTANT PROVISIONS

Fire precautions and prevention. Section 40. Any factory which (a) has more than 20 persons employed or (b) has more than 10 persons employed above the ground floor or (c) has inflammable or explosive materials used or stored must obtain a certificate from the fire authorities stating that the premises has means of escape as should reasonably be required in case of fire. Such escape routes shall be properly maintained and free from obstruction. Fire exits shall be conspicuously marked, doors must not be locked so that they cannot be opened from the inside, and must open outwards (unless they are sliding doors). There must be proper and audible fire warnings which must be tested at least every three months, and the test must be recorded in the general register.

First Aid. Section 61

(i) A first aid box or cupboard of prescribed standard must be provided, and be readily accessible. It must contain nothing but first aid appliances or requisites. If there are more than 150 persons employed, an additional box must be provided for each additional 150 employees.

(ii) Each box or cupboard must be in charge of a responsible person. If more than 50 persons are employed, that person must have received training in first aid, and always be available during working hours.

(iii) Every workroom must contain a notice stating the name of the person who is in charge of first aid.

(iv) The chief inspector may exempt firms from certain of these requirements if the firm has an ambulance room, wherein all injuries can be treated.

7. WELFARE

Section 57. There must be an adequate supply of drinking water, which, if not laid on from a public main, must be in suitable vessels and renewed daily. Washing facilities must be provided, with soap and clean towels (or other suitable methods) and clean hot and cold running water. The washing facilities must be cleaned and kept tidy. Suitable accommodation for clothing not worn during working hours must be provided (*McCarthy* v. *Daily Mirror* (1949)) and drying facilities made available where practicable. If workpeople can do their work properly while seated, suitable seating must be provided.

Special Provisions:

Section 63. This deals with the prevention dust and fumes (*Graham* v. *C.W.S.* (1947)), (section 4 deals with the circulation of fresh air) and all practicable steps must be taken to prevent employees inhaling dust, fumes or impurities, but this duty does not arise if it is not known that there is a danger in so inhaling: *Richards* v. *Highway Ironfounders* (1955).

8. NOTIFICATION AND INVESTIGATION OF ACCIDENTS AND INDUSTRIAL DISEASES

Section 80. Any accident which causes death or disables an employee from earning full wages for more than three days at his usual work shall be reported to the District Inspector.

Certain specified accidents must be reported even though no one is injured, including electrical short circuits, certain explosions or fires, collapse or failure of a crane or hoist, etc.

Certain industrial diseases must be reported to the Chief Inspector of Factories by any medical practitioner who treats an affected person, as well as by the employer to the district inspector and the factory doctor.

The factory inspector must be present at any inquest on a person killed by an industrial accident or disease.

The Minister has power to direct that a formal enquiry takes place and the investigation has the same powers of hearing as a magistrates' Court.

9. EMPLOYMENT OF WOMEN AND YOUNG PERSONS

(a) *Working conditions*: They may not clean any part of a prime mover or transmission machinery while it is in motion, or clean any part of any machine if this would expose them to the risk of injury from any moving part or any adjacent machinery (Section 20). Certain machines may be prescribed by the Minister as being dangerous, and a young person may not work on them unless he has been adequately trained or is working under supervision (section 21).

No person may carry or lift a load so heavy as being likely to cause him injury (section 72). Female young persons may not work in part of a factory where certain glass blowing processes are being carried out and lead components are being used (ss. 73-75).

Young persons under the age of 16 must be examined by the appointed factory doctor, who must certify their fitness for the employment. The certificate may make conditions as to the kind of work on which the young person concerned may be employed; section 118.

(b) *Hours of work*: Total hours of work excluding intervals allowed for meals and rest must not exceed 9 in any day nor exceed 48 in any week (44 hours in the case of a young person under 16). *The period of employment* must not exceed 11 hours in any day; it must not begin earlier than 7 a.m. nor end later than 6 p.m. for persons under 16—8 p.m. for persons under 18 and for women. Work must end at 1 p.m. on Saturday.

The maximum continuous spell of work must not be longer than $4\frac{1}{2}$ hours without a break of at least 30 minutes, though this may be increased to 5 hours if there is a break of at least 10 minutes in that time. A notice of the hours of work and rest and meal period must be posted in the factory (s. 88).

In special circumstances it is possible for women and young persons to work overtime, but this must not be more than 6 hours per week, nor more than 100 hours per year. The total hours worked shall not exceed more than 10 hours per day ($10\frac{1}{2}$ hours if a five-day week is being worked); the period within which overtime is being worked must not exceed 25 weeks per year. The Minister may make regulations in certain circumstances (mainly in connection with seasonal trades). Shift work is permissible if the Minister so authorises, but the consent of the majority of the employees must be obtained by a secret ballot. There are exceptions for women employed in managerial positions and the Minister may suspend these requirements in emergency situations. General or Special exemption orders may be applied for and made by the Minister.

Notices and Returns

One month before occupation, the occupier must send a notice to the inspector of his intention to occupy the premises, informing him whether or not any mechanical power is being used (s. 137).

An abstract of the Act shall be posted at the principal entrances of the factory.
There shall also be similarly posted:

    (i) a notice of the address of the district and divisional inspectors

    (ii) a notice with the name and address of the appointed factory doctor

    (iii) a notice specifying the clock by which employment and intervals in the factory are to be regulated

    (iv) any other notices required by the Act (s. 138).

The abstract and the notices shall be in such characters and in such positions as to be conveniently read by persons employed in the factory.

Every factory must have a general register, which must contain the following particulars:

(i) details of young person employed

(ii) particulars as to the washing, whitewashing, varnishing, painting, etc. of the factory as required by s. 1.

(iii) particulars of every accident and industrial disease.

(iv) details of any special exemptions of which the occupier has availed himself (e.g. 99;113) and anything else required to be entered in the register e.g. testing of fire warnings. Attached to the general register must be all reports and particulars required by the Act, e.g. fire authority's certificate, and other matters that the Minister may prescribe. (s. 140).

10. OBSERVANCE OF THE ACT

Five classes of persons may be liable for offences for breach of the Act:

(i) The occupier is the person primarily responsible, both civilly and criminally. Fines of up to £300 can be imposed for a criminal offence. He can defend himself by showing that: (1) he used all diligence to enforce the Act *Land* (2) the offence was committed without his knowledge, consent, connivance or fault (s. 161).

(ii) The owner of a tenement factory will be liable in certain circumstances (ss. 120-122) for matters which fall within his control. He has the same defences as the occupier.

(iii) The owner or seller or hirer of a machine will be liable unless it is so constructed as to prevent an injury (ss. 17, 163).

Biddle v. *Truvox Engineering Co.* (1952)

An injured workman sued his employers and the manufacturers of a machine which had not been securely fenced.

Held, the Act did not confer the right of a civil action on the injured workman against the manufacturer, but only imposed a criminal penalty on the seller of the machine.

(iv) An employee will be liable if he wilfully misuses or interferes with anything securing the health, safety or welfare of persons employed in the factory. He must use all safety precautions and must not do anything liable to injure anyone (s. 143).

An employer may not make any deductions from wages to pay for anything he has to do under the Act, nor permit one employee to receive payment from another (s. 136).

(v) Officers of the company are liable if the offence is committed with their connivance or consent, or through their negligence.

11. ADMINISTRATION

The administration of the Act is in the hands of four separate bodies.

(i) *Factory Inspectorate.* Under the general control of the Department of Employment and Productivity as many factory Inspectors as necessary are appointed. Their powers are

- (a) to enter and examine and inspect at all reasonable times by day or night, any factory
- (b) To take a police officer with them if they apprehend serious obstruction in the course of their duty.
- (c) To require the production of register, notices, certificates.
- (d) To make such enquiry and examination as may be necessary to ascertain whether or not the provisions of the Act are being complied with.
- (e) To examine and question any employee in the factory.
- (f) To take a medical officer of health or a sanitary officer with them.
- (g) Inspect premises before they are to be used.
- (h) To bring proceedings under the Act (s. 146).

The wilful obstruction or delay of an inspector or the withholding of information are offences.

(*ii*) *Fire Authorities*

Have a like power of entry and inspection for fire purposes (section 148).

(*iii*) *Factory doctors*

A sufficient number may be appointed. They can—

- (a) examine young persons
- (b) investigate and report on certain accidents and industrial diseases
- (c) prevent certain persons from being employed in the factory (s. 151).

(*iv*) *Local Authorities* are responsible for

- (a) sanitary provisions (whether there is mechanical power or not) (s. 8 (1)).
- (b) cleanliness, overcrowding temperature, ventilation and drainage where there is no mechanical power (s. 8 (2)).

(c) Homeworkers. A list must be sent to Local Authority twice a year (s. 133).

If the factory inspectorate inform the Local Authorities of a defect or default falling within their sphere, the council must see that it is remedied within one month, or the Inspectorate may institute proceedings (s. 9.).

2. Offices, Shops and Railway Premises Act 1963

The Act applies to offices, shops and railway premises (with certain exceptions) where persons are employed to work.

(i) Office premises means a building or part of a building which is solely or principally used for office purposes. This includes administration, clerical work, handling money, telephone or telegraph services.

(ii) Shops include a building or part of a building which is not a shop but which is used principally or solely for the retail trade or business.

(iii) Railway premises means a building occupied by railway undertakers for the purpose of the railway undertaking and situate in the vicinity of the permanent way.

The Act does *not* include.

(a) premises where self-employed person work;
(b) premises where only the employer's relations work;
(c) dwellings of outworkers;
(d) premises where people work less than 21 hours per week;
(e) premises of a temporary nature (six months for a moveable structure, and six weeks in other cases).

The main provisions of the Act are

(i) All premises and furniture must be kept clean; the floors and steps must be cleaned at least once a week.

(ii) A room where people are working must not be so overcrowded so as to cause a risk of injury to health.

(iii) A reasonable temperature must be maintained, and a thermometer provided in a conspicuous place on each floor.

(iv) Effective and suitable provision must be made for securing the ventilation of every room.

(v) Lighting, whether natural or artificial, must be suitable and sufficient.

(vi) Sanitary conveniences must be provided, and kept clean and properly maintained.

(vii) Washing facilities must be provided, with clean hot and cold running water, soap and drying facilities.

(viii) Drinking water must be provided.

(ix) Accommodation for clothing must be provided with drying facilities.

(x) Where people have a reasonable opportunity for sitting down during their work, suitable facilities must be provided.

(xi) Eating facilities must be provided for persons who eat meals in shops.

(xii) Floors, passages, stairs, etc. must be soundly constructed and properly maintained, and must, so far as is reasonably practicable be kept free from obstructions and slippery substances. A substantial handrail must be provided with every staircase.

(xiii) Every dangerous part of any machinery must be securely fenced.

(xiv) No young person may clean machinery if this exposes him to the risk of injury.

(xv) Training and supervision must be provided for anyone working on a machine prescribed as dangerous.

(xvi) No person shall be required to lift any load so heavy as to be likely to cause him injury.

(xvii) A first aid box or cupboard must be readily accessible. Where more than 150 are employed an additional box shall be provided for each further 150 employees and a competent person trained in first aid shall be in charge.

(xviii) All premises must have reasonably adequate means of escape in case of fire.

(xix) Every employee must have a free passageway in the event of fire, and all doors must be easily opened.

(xx) Fire fighting equipment must be provided and maintained, fire alarms maintained and tested, fire exits marked, and fire drill practised. A fire certificate must be applied for in any premises where more than 20 persons are employed, or more than 10 employed above the ground floor.

(xxi) Notification of accidents. If an accident causes (1) death, or (2) disables an employee from doing his work for more than three days, it must be reported.

(xxii) Exemptions. The Act empowers the Minister and the enforcing authority to grant exemptions in certain cases.

LIABILITY UNDER THE ACT

The responsibility to ensure compliance with the Act lies on the occupier, the employer and the owner of the building. Further, any person who wilfully and without reasonable cause does anything to endanger the health or safety of employees commits an offence. It is a defence under the Act to show that the person prosecuted has used all diligence to ensure compliance with the Act.

ENFORCEMENT OF THE ACT

Local Authorities have the duty of enforcing the Act within their area but responsibility for inspecting premises is under the Factory Inspectorate.

They have the same powers as are conferred by the Factories Act. Fire authorities enforce the provisions relating to fire precautions.

Chapter 3
Trade Unions and the Law

1. Definition

A trade union is any combination, whether temporary or permanent, the principal objects of which are statutory objects, namely, the regulation of relations between employers and employees, or employers and employers, or employees and employees, or the imposing of any restrictive conditions on the conduct of any trade or business. (Trade Union Acts 1871–1913). Although a trade union is commonly thought of as being an organisation of employees, the statutory definition clearly includes employers' associations (*Chamberlain's Wharf* v. *Smith* (1913).) if their principal objects are statutory objects, though not if on the whole they are trade associations.

> *Performing Rights Society* v. *London Theatre of Varieties* (1924).
> The principle objects of the appellant society was the protection of copyrights. It could also impose restrictive conditions on the conduct of the industry.
> *Held* the society was not a trade union. The imposition of restrictive conditions was ancilliary to its main objects.

2. Legal Status

THE DOCTRINE OF RESTRAINT OF TRADE

If a trade union has objects which are in restraint of trade it is an unlawful body at common law; *Russell* v. *Amalgamated Society of Carpenters and Joiners* (1912). However s. 3 of the Trade Union Act 1871 provides that merely because a trade union has such unlawful objects, this will not invalidate any agreement or trust. (See however s. 4 of the Act, below).

A trade union which does not have objects which are in restraint of trade is a perfectly lawful body at common law: *Osborne* v. *Amalgamated Society of Railway Servants* (1911).

The incorporation of a trade union under the Companies Act is prohibited (Trade Union Act 1871, s. 5) and any such incorporation is clearly void, despite the conclusiveness of the certificate of incorporation: *British Association of Glass Bottle Manufacturers* v. *Nettlefolds* (1911). In law, therefore, a trade union is merely an unincorporate association. However, a trade union may be registered, unregistered, or certified.

REGISTERED TRADE UNIONS

Any trade union of seven or more members may register with the Registrar of Friendly Societies, by submitting two copies of its rules. These must contain

(i) the name and the place of meeting

(ii) the objects of the union, specifying those objects on which union funds may be spent

(iii) the benefits which are available to members

(iv) details of fines which may be imposed

(v) the method of altering its rules

(vi) the appointment of the committee of management, trustees and officials

(vii) details of auditing of accounts, investment of funds, and the inspection of the books by members.

The Registrar may refuse the registration if (i) the principal objects are not statutory objects, (ii) the objects are unlawful, or (iii) the name resembles too closely the name of another registered union. The fact that the Registrar has approved the rules is not conclusive, and if they are unlawful they may be challenged despite registration: *Birch* v. *N.U.R.* (1950), *infra*.

Registration is voluntary and most Employers' Associations have failed to register. Nonetheless, nearly all of the employee trade unions seem to have done so, and have thus obtained the following advantages which registration brings about:

(a) On the change of trustees, the property of the union automatically vests in the new trustees.

(b) Certain income tax benefits accrue in respect of dividends and interest earned on union investments.

(c) A registered trade union may sue or be sued in its own name, without requiring resort to representative actions.

(d) Disorderly conduct in its library may be an offence under the Libraries Offences Act 1898

(e) The treasurer can be compelled to provide the trustees or the members with an account of all expenditure and receipts, and summary proceedings can be taken to recover property wrongfully applied.

(f) A member of a registered trade union may nominate the name of a person to receive a death benefit payable by the union.

The effect of registration is that a statutory legal entity is created (*Taff Vale Railway Co.* v. *A.S.R.S.* (1901)), which has a legal personality capable of suing (*National Union of General and Municipal Workers* v. *Gillian* (1945)) and being sued: *Bonsor* v. *Musicians' Union* (1956).

UNREGISTERED TRADE UNIONS are unincorporate associations, and any action by or against them must be brought in the names of trustees or a representative action under Order 15, rule 12 of the Rules of the Supreme Court. However, they are still entitled to the benefits conferred by the Trade Union Acts and the Trade Disputes Acts.

CERTIFIED UNIONS—Any trade union may apply to the Registrar for a certificate that it is a trade union within the meaning of the Acts (Trade Union Act 1913 s. 2 (3)). The Registrar must grant the certificates if he is satisfied that the union is being carried on for the purposes of the statutory objects, but he may withdraw it if the certificate is no longer justified. While it is in force, it is conclusive for all purposes that the union is a trade union within the meaning of the Acts. It would seem, therefore, that a certified trade union may sue and be sued in its certified name.

3. Membership of a Trade Union

In general, a trade union itself can lay down in its rules who is eligible for membership.

Boulting Bros. v. *A.C.T.A.T.* (1963)

The plaintiffs were the managing directors of a film company, and also worked on the technical side of producing films. They resigned from the defendant union, who resorted to industrial action to compel them to rejoin. The plaintiffs brought an action against the union, claiming that they were ineligible for membership.

Held, the fact that they exercised employees' functions on the production floor meant that they were eligible within the rules.

The rules can prescribe a class of persons who are not eligible.

Faramus v. *Film Artistes' Association* (1964)

The rules of a trade union provided that no person convicted of a criminal offence (other than minor motoring effences) was eligible to join or remain a member of the union. The plaintiff had, many years previously, been convicted of two offences in Jersey while that country was occupied by Germany during the war.

Held, his admission to the union was a nullity.

If they do not provide for a certain class of members, a person who purports to join as a member of that class has never been a member.

Martin v. *Scottish Transport & General Workers' Union* (1952)

The plaintiff was admitted to the union as a temporary member. He was subsequently informed that this membership had been revoked. He brought an action for a declaration that he was still a member.

Held, as the union rules did not provide for temporary membership, his admission to the union was a nullity.

A court has no power to order admission to membership (*Byrne* v. *Kinomatograph Renters* (1959)), but a rule which arbitrarily restricts membership may be void as being against public policy.

Nagle v. *Feilden* (1966)

It was the unwritten policy of the Jockey Club not to grant training licences to women. The plaintiff sued the stewards for a declaration that this "unwritten rule" was contrary to public policy.

> *Held*, at common law a person had a right to work at his (or her) trade or profession without being arbitrarily and unreasonably excluded from it.

Further, if the motives for refusing admission are wrongful (e.g. spite or prejudice) an actionable conspiracy may exist: *Crofter Hand Woven Harris Tweed* v. *Veitch* (1942) *per* LORD PORTER.

4. Effect of Union Rules

The rules constitute a contract between the union and its members, and therefore, they must be strictly adhered to.

> *Yorkshire Miners' Association* v. *Howden* (1905)
>
> A trade union made strike payments to members contrary to the strict rules of the union.
> *Held*, the payments were wrongfully paid.

However, by s. 4 of the 1871 Act, certain contracts entered into by a union which has rules which are in restraint of trade at common law are unenforceable directly. These are

(1) any agreement concerning the conditions on which members shall sell or not sell goods, transact business, employ or be employed;

(2) any agreement for the payment of a subscription or a penalty;

(3) any agreement for the application of trade union funds to provide benefits, make a payment to an employer or workman who is not a member, in consideration of him acting in conformity with the rules or a resolution of the union, or any agreement to discharge a fine imposed by a court of law;

(4) any agreement between one trade union and another, and

(5) any bond to secure the performance of any of these agreements.

The section does not prevent an action to enforce any of these agreements in an indirect manner (*Y.M.A.* v. *Howden, supra*) nor does it prevent a declaration being sought as to the meaning or interpretation of the rules.

If the rules provide that a member shall receive legal assistance, the union fulfills that obligation by taking expert legal advice on the matter on behalf of the member.

Cross v. *British Iron, Steel & Kindred Trades Association* (1968)

The rules of the union provided that legal assistance would be given to members in certain circumstances. The plaintiff sustained an accident at work, and gave details to the branch secretary. These were forwarded to a solicitor, who advised that the plaintiff had no case. The action then became statute barred. The plaintiff sued the union for negligence.

Held, the union had performed its duty by submitting the case to a competent solicitor. There was no duty to inform the plaintiff of the three year limitation period.

Nor is the union in breach of contract if the member fails to show that his action had a reasonable prospect of success.

Buckley v. *National Union of General & Municipal Workers* (1967)

The plaintiff sustained an accident at work. She informed the local union official of the facts, who thought that she had no prospect of bringing a successful action. She was not informed that her action would be statute barred after three years. She sued the union for breach of contract, and the union official for negligence.

Held, the union had not broken its contractual obligation, and the official had not been negligent.

A trade union has implied powers to spend money on things which are incidental to achieving its objects, such as making payments to salaried officials, and paying costs incurred in litigation which arise out of their work.

Hill v. *Archbold* (1967)

Two union officials brought libel actions which arose out of their employment. The actions were dismissed, but the union sought to pay the costs on behalf of the officials. The rules did not provide for this.

Held, the union had implied power to pay the costs, for the matter was incidental to the work of the officials on behalf of the union.

5. Expulsion from Membership

A trade union may only expel a person from membership if such power exists in its rules.

Spring v. *National Amalgamated Stevedores & Dockers' Society* (1956)

The Trades Union Congress propounded an agreement (the Bridlington Agreement) designed to prevent unions from poaching each other's members. Contrary to this agreement, the defendant union enrolled the plaintiff as a member. The union was then ordered by the T.U.C. to expel him, which it did, but the rules of the union contained no power of expulsion.

Held, the expulsion was void.

If the union rules confer a power of expulsion on certain specified grounds, a member may only be expelled for a breach of that specific rule, and not for any other reasons. Moreover, the court will decide whether or not the member was in fact in breach of that rule, and will if necessary substitute its own opinion for that of the union.

Lee v. *Showman's Guild of Great Britain* (1952)

The plaintiff was expelled from the defendant Guild for violating a rule designed to prevent unfair competition.

Held, the courts had jurisdiction to examine the meaning of the rules, and since the Guild had misconstrued the meaning of the term "unfair competitition", the expulsion was void.

This is particularly so when the rules are vague (e.g. "conduct detrimental to the union" (*Kelly* v. *Natsopa* (1915)), though if the court decides that the violation by the member was serious, they will uphold the expulsion.

Evans v. *National Union of Printing, Bookbinding and Paper Workers* (1938)

The union's rules provided that a member who acted contrary to the union's interests may be expelled. The plaintiff absented himself from work on several occasions, contrary to an agreement between the union and the employers. As a result of such conduct, the union expelled him from membership.

Held, the expulsion was valid.

The union rules cannot be so framed as to oust the jurisdiction of the courts by making the decision of the union binding and final: *Chapple* v. *Electrical Trades Union* (1960). If the expulsion is made under rules which provide for a right of appeal and that right is subsequently taken away, the expulsion will be invalid.

Braithwaite v. *Electrical Electronics and Telecommunication Union* (1969)

The plaintiff was expelled in February, and his appeal was to be heard in October. Before then, the union amalgamated with another, and the new rules contained no provision for pending appeals. The new union sought to deal with the matter the following January.

Held, the expulsion was invalid. The new appeals committee had no jurisdiction to deal with the matter, and the plaintiff was denied membership of the union for three months longer than necessary. Because his right of appeal had been taken away, even though it was through an oversight, the expulsion was ineffective. The expulsion must be for the benefit of the union, not an individual.

Abbott v. *Sullivan* (1952)

The plaintiff was fined by a disciplinary committee. Immediately after the meeting, he struck one of the officials, who reconvened the committee, which expelled the plaintiff.

Held, the expulsion was void.

PROCEDURE FOR EXPULSION

If the union rules provide for a certain procedure to be adopted, then this must be strictly followed and adhered to, and the smallest irregularity will be as fatal as the greatest. But if the rules provide for an internal appeal within the union machinery, that remedy must be pursued before recourse can be had to the courts.

White v. *Kuzych* (1951)

The appellant was expelled from a union. The rules provided that an appeal against such a decision could be made to the union's executive. The appellant brought an action for a declaration that his expulsion was void.

Held, the action must fail. He should have exhausted all the internal remedies provided by the rules before he could bring an action at law.

On the other hand, if the purported expulsion is void because of lack of authority or other reason, then, as the union appeal machinery cannot cure the defect, the member may appeal to the court without exhausting the internal machinery.

Annamunthodo v. *Oilfields Workers' Trade Union* (1961)

The appellant was charged with certain offences, contrary to the union rules. He denied the charges, and the meeting was adjourned. At a subsequent hearing, which he did not attend, different charges were presented, and he was expelled.

Held, the expulsion was void *ab initio.* The appellant should have been given notice of the new charges, and failure to do so meant that the union was acting ultra vires.

Natural justice. Since the union is exercising a quasi-judicial function, it is thought that the rules of natural justice apply in these circumstances. If the union has powers which enable them to expel a member without a hearing, or without knowing of the charge against him, the better view is that such rules are void: *per* DENNING, L. J. in *Russell* v. *Norfolk* (1949).

Lawlor v. *Union of Post Office Workers* (1965)

The rules of the union provided that "any member shall be expelled from the union who in the opinion of the executive council is not a fit and proper person for membership." Other rules provided for an appeal machinery. The plaintiff was expelled without being told the nature of the charges, and without an opportunity to be heard in his own defence.

Held, the rules predicated an enquiry of a judicial nature, and the rules of natural justice must be implied into them. Since these rules has been violated, the expulsion was void.

The fact that the body charged with the task of hearing the case is biased is not relevant as long as they act fairly and within the true meaning of the rules.

MacLean v. *Workers' Union* (1929)

The plaintiff was expelled from the union for issuing circulars

E

which criticised the conduct of the executive committee. The committee itself resolved to expel him, after giving him a due hearing.

Held, the expulsion was in accordance with the rules, and was valid. The committee had acted honestly and in good faith.

REMEDY FOR WRONGFUL EXPULSION

A member wrongfully expelled may apply for a declaration that he is still a member, he may apply for an injunction restraining the union from acting on the expulsion, and since the rules of the union are a contract between the union and the member, he may bring an action for damages for wrongful expulsion.

Bonsor v. *Musician's Union* (1956)

The appellant was expelled by the branch secretary of a registered union. The power of expulsion could only be exercised by the branch committee.

Held, the expulsion was void, and he could recover damages for wrongful expulsion.

NOTE: The House of Lords disagreed as to the basis for liability. Two Law Lords thought that the union was a distinct legal entity, which had broken *its* contract with the appellant. Two other Law Lords thought that the rules were a contract between the members *inter se* and these members were liable for the wrongful acts of their agent, i.e. the branch secretary. The meaning of the speech of the fifth Law Lord is unclear.

6. Political Activities.

A trade union may engage in political activities if its members pass a resolution by a majority of those voting establishing political objects as one of its objects. The rules must be approved by the Registrar, and must contain the following—

  (a) A special political fund must be set up, separate from the general funds of the union
  (b) Any member who does not wish to contribute may contract out
  (c) A member who contracts out of the political fund shall not be excluded from any benefit or disqualified from holding

any office except a position connected with the management of the political fund.

Birch v. *National Union of Railwaymen* (1950)

The rules of a union provided that a member who contracted out could not be elected to an office which involved management of the political fund. The plaintiff was elected branch chairman, but the union declared him to be ineligible for the office, because it involved control over the political fund, and he had contracted out. The rules of the union had been approved by the Registrar.

Held, the rules violated the Act, and the plaintiff was entitled to a declaration.

(d) Contributing to the political fund must not be a condition of membership of the union.

THE POLITICAL OBJECTS IN WHICH A UNION MAY ENGAGE ARE:—

(i) the payment of the expenses of a candidate for parliamentary or other public office;

(ii) the holding of meetings or distribution of literature for such candidates;

(iii) the maintenance of such person holding such office;

(iv) the registration of electors or the selection of such candidates;

(v) the general distribution of election literature.

Chapter 4 *The Law and Industrial Relations*

1. Collective Bargaining

A collective agreement is an agreement made between a trade union on the one hand, and an employer or an employers' association on the other, which lays down the terms and conditions of employment of employees. There is, however, no legal duty on an employer to recognise a union (*Thomson* v. *Deakin* (1952)), or even to bargain with it: *Stratford* v. *Lindley* (1964). Certain statutory authorities, such as the nationalised industries, have been placed under statutory obligations to "enter into" or "to seek" consultation with appropriate trade unions, (see Coal Industry Nationalisation Act 1946, s. 46, Transport Act 1962. s. 72. Gas Act 1948, s. 57, Electricity Act 1957, s. 12, Air Corporations Act 1949, s. 20), but it is not thought that such obligations are readily enforced.

LEGAL ENFORCEMENT OF COLLECTIVE AGREEMENTS

(i) A federated agreement (i.e. made between a trade union and an employers association) is not unlawful merely because the union has objects which are in restraint of trade (s. 3 Trade Union Act 1871) but s. 4 (4) of the Act provides that nothing in the Act (i.e. referring to s. 3) shall enable the courts directly to enforce any agreement between one trade union and another. Since an employers' association may be a trade union by definition (see above) some collective agreements are caught by this restriction. However, the limitations of the section should be noted: (a) It does not apply if the trade unions are not bodies in restraint of trade, for then no reliance is placed on s. 3 for the validation of the agreement, and "nothing in the Act" is being relied upon for its validity. (b) The Act does not prohibit the indirect enforcement of the agreements mentioned in section 4, such as an action for a declaration, or (possibly) an injunction to restrain a breach. (c) A number of employers' associations are probably not in fact trade unions by the legal definition, for their principal objects are not the statutory objects. If so, the agreement is not one between one trade union and another.

(ii) The Plant agreement (i.e. made between a single employer and a trade union). This agreement is not caught by the provisions of s. 4 (4), and may therefore, be legally binding.

Bradford Dyers' Association v. *Amalgamated Society of Dyers, Bleachers and Finishers* (1926)

The plaintiffs signed an agreement with three trade unions which contained, inter alia, a "no strike" clause. In breach of this agreement, the unions called a strike. In an action by the plaintiffs against the unions, the latter admitted that the agreement was binding on them, and consented to judgment, nominal damages being awarded to the plaintiffs.

However, if the parties do not intend to be legally bound to an agreement they may exclude such liability: *Rose and Frank* v. *Crompton Bros.* (1923). The climate of opinion as evidenced by contemporary sources may indicate that the parties do not intend to be legally bound.

Ford Motor Co. v. *Amalgamated Union of Engineering & Foundry Workers* (1969)

The plaintiffs sued two unions for breach of an agreement not to strike.

Held, the agreement was not intended to be legally binding.

The "normative" aspect of collective agreements

The importance of collective agreements lies in the fact that some of their terms become incorporated into the individual contract of employment, either expressly or impliedly (see above, page 14). Moreover, there are two further ways in which collective agreements may be relevant to the individual employee.

(i) The Terms and Conditions of Employment Act 1959—Section 8. If a claim is reported to the Minister that in a particular industry the terms of conditions of employment have been settled by bodies which represent both sides of industry, and that a particular employer is not observing those terms, the Minister, if he cannot otherwise settle the claim, must refer the matter to the Industrial Court. If this body finds the claim well founded, it may make an award requiring the employer to observe those terms and conditions which are thus implied into the individual contract of employment. Only organisations which are party to the collective agreement may report such a claim.

(ii) Fair Wages Clause

By a resolution of the House of Commons passed in 1946, a clause must be inserted in all Government contracts to the effect that any contractor

(a) must pay wages and observe the conditions of employment no less favourable than those commonly accepted in the district, or observed by other employers in the industry in similar circumstances.

(b) He must comply with this provision in respect of all his workers, and not just those engaged on the contract, and before being placed on the list of firms invited to tender for Government contracts, he must show that he has observed those terms and conditions for at least the preceding three months.

(c) The contractor must recognise freedom of his workmen to join trade unions.

(d) A copy of the resolution must be displayed in the workplace during the continuance of the contract.

(e) The contractor must ensure the observance of the terms of the resolution by any sub-contractor employed by him. Any dispute as to the observance of the resolution must be referred to the Minister, who, if the matter is not otherwise settled, must refer the matter to arbitration (usually by the Industrial Court).

2. Industrial Disputes

A strike normally amounts to a breach of contract by the individual employee, though not if notice of strike action is given which is longer than the notice required to terminate the employment.

Morgan v. *Fry* (1968)

A trade union official told the employer on 14th March that unless the plaintiff re-joined the union by 1st April the men would not work with him. The workmen could terminate their contracts of employment by giving one week's notice. The plaintiff was dismissed, and he brought an action for conspiracy and intimidation.

Held, no unlawful act had been committed by the union or the workmen.

However, there are four other headings of legal liability which must be considered, together with the various defences which may be raised. There are also statutory provisions which provide protection to trade unions and their members in appropriate circumstances.

1. CONSPIRACY—A conspiracy is any combination of two or more persons to do an unlawful act, or a lawful act by unlawful means. One person, acting alone, cannot be guilty of a conspiracy: *Allen* v. *Flood* (1898). The unlawful act in trade disputes is one designed to do harm to a person in his trade or business.

Quinn v. *Leatham* (1901)

Union officials demanded that the Leatham should dismiss certain employees who were non-unionists. He refused to do so, but offered to pay their subscription arrears if the union would admit them to membership. The union refused as they wished to "teach them a lesson". The union then approached a customer of Leatham, and under threats of strike action, got him to stop dealing with Leatham.

Held, the union officials were guilty of civil conspiracy.

The fact that harm is caused is irrelevant if the combination are pursuing their own legitimate aims.

Crofter Hand Woven Harris Tweed v. *Veitch* (1942)

The union wanted to secure a wage increase for its members employed in the weaving mills on the island of Lewes. The employers refused the claim, pointing out that they were

using an expensive yarn woven by local crofters, and had
to compete with local weavers who were importing cheaper
yarn from the mainland. The union therefore advised its
dock workers to place an embargo on yarn going to local
weavers.

Held, the union was pursuing its *legitimate* interests. The
fact that harm was being caused to local weavers did not
make the activities of the union unlawful.

A conspiracy, therefore, does not exist if the union is pursuing
its genuine legitimate interests, which include attempts to enforce
a closed shop (*Reynolds* v. *Shipping Federation* (1924)), opposing
a colour bar (*Scala Ballroom* v. *Ratcliffe* (1958)), protecting members
from defaulting employers (*Dean* v. *Craik* (1962)), striking for
higher wages (*per* LORD BRAMWELL in *Mogul Steamship Co.* v.
McGregor Gow & Co. (1892)), refusing to work with non-unionists
(*Wolstenholme* v. *Arris* (1920)), and threatening to strike unless a
non-unionist is dismissed (*Santan* v. *Busnach* (1913)). But a conspiracy which is pursued merely to further a grudge is actionable
as is one in which unlawful means are used: *Rookes* v. *Barnard*
(1964), (see below).

Huntley v. *Thornton* (1957)

The plaintiff was involved in a dispute with local trade union
officials, who purported to expel him. The expulsion was not
upheld by the national executive committee. Nonetheless, the
local officials regarded him as no longer being a member, and
took steps to ensure that he could not get a job.

Held, the officials were liable for conspiracy. They were
pursuing a personal grudge, not legitimate trade union
objectives.

2. INDUCING A BREACH OF CONTRACT—It is a tort to induce
someone to break, or to procure a breach of, an existing contract:
Lumley v. *Gye* (1853).

There are five elements to this tort. There must be
(1) knowledge of the contract,
(2) an intention to induce or procure the breach,
(3) an act of inducement or procurement,
(4) a breach which flows as a natural consequence of that act,
(5) no justification for inducing or procuring the breach.

So far as industrial disputes are concerned, there are two circumstances which may give rise to this tort.

(a) *Inducing a breach of a subsisting contract of employment.* Whenever a trade union official calls a strike, he is inducing a breach of a contract of employment.

South Wales Miners' Federation v. *Glamorgan Coal Co.* (1905)

A union called a strike in order to obtain higher wages. *Held,* they were liable for damages. The fact that they were acting in furtherance of their own interests was irrelevant.

So too, a union official who asks his members to provide him with confidential information about the employer's business is procuring a breach of that contract: *Bents Brewery* v. *Hogan* (1945). However, a breach is not being induced if notice is given which is longer than the notice required to terminate the contract: *Morgan* v. *Fry* (1968) (*supra*).

It is a defence to this action to show that that there was justification for inducing the breach.

Brimlow v. *Casson* (1924)

The defendant induced theatre owners to break their contracts with a theatrical producer, who was paying wages which were so low that his chorus girls had to resort to prostitution in order to make a living. *Held,* the defendant's action was justified.

(b) *Inducing the breach of a commercial contract.* This is where the union attempts a secondary boycott, or uses other indirect pressure: *Thomson* v. *Deakin* (1952). There must be knowledge of the existence of the contract the breach of which it is hoped to induce or procure, but this does not require specific or detailed knowledge.

Emerald Construction Co. v. *Lothian* (1966)

Building contractors contracted with the plaintiffs for the supply of labour on a building site. The union, which objected to "labour only" sub-contracts, tried to terminate this contract by industrial action. *Held,* an interlocutory injunction would lie to restrain the defendants from attempting to procure a breach of the contract between the plaintiffs and the building contractors.

It is enough if the inducer acted without caring whether he induced a breach or not: *Daily Mirror Newspapers* v. *Gardner* (1968).

3. INTIMIDATION—If the industrial action is not lawful, it follows that a wrongful act has been committed. Since a strike is *prima facie* a breach of contract, then it is not lawful, and a threat to strike thus becomes actionable as being the tort of intimidation.

Rookes v. *Barnard* (1964)

The defendants, who objected to the continued employment of the plaintiff, a non-unionist, informed the employer that there would be a strike unless he was dismissed. The employers lawfully terminated the plaintiff's employment.

Held, the threat to strike was the threat of an unlawful act i.e. it was a threat to break their own contracts of employment, and was thus actionable.

The essence of this tort is "any menacing action or language the influence of which no ordinary firmness or strength of mind can reasonably be expected to resist" *per* HAWKINS, J. in *Allen* v. *Flood* (1898). Presumably it is a question of fact whether or not the person intimidated ought to have resisted. Intimidation may be against the plaintiff himself (e.g. a threat to slash the tyres of the car belonging to a non-unionist) or against a third party who is forced to act to the detriment of the plaintiff: *Rookes* v. *Barnard* (*ante*). A threat, however, is only actionable if it is a threat to do something which is wrongful, e.g. to commit a crime, or a tort, or a breach of contract. The difficulty is to distinguish a "threat" from "merely informing" (*White* v. *Riley* (1921)) or "communicating to" the employer the consequences which may flow from his continuing employment of a non-unionist: *Hodges* v. *Webb* (1920).

4. RESIDUAL TORTIOUS LIABILITY—Recent cases have suggested that there may well be further legal developments in this area of the law. In particular, it has been suggested that:

(a) The mere interference with business, if done maliciously, could be tortious, even if such act is done by one person: *per*

LORD DEVLIN in *Rookes* v. *Barnard* (1964). Since the House of Lords are no longer bound by their own decisions, it would be possible to circumvent *Allen* v. *Flood* on this point. (But see also Trade Disputes Act 1965, *infra*).

(b) Conspiracy to break a contract based on a revival of cases like R. v. *Bunn* (1872). Since a breach of contract is unlawful, a conspiracy to do so must *a fortriori* be a conspiracy to do an unlawful act.

(c) Interference by unlawful means with future contracts (*Stratford* v. *Lindley* (1964)) caused by inducing the breach of employment contracts.

3. Statutory Defences

IMMUNITY OF TRADE UNIONS FROM ACTIONS IN TORT—Section 4 of the Trade Disputes Act 1906 provides that no action against a trade union in respect of any tortious act alleged to have been committed shall be entertained by any court. The section covers all tortious acts, not just those committed in the course of a trade dispute (*Vacher* v. *London Society of Compositors* (1913)), but does not cover actions concerning the property of a trade union (subsections 2) (thus an action for nuisance committed on trade union premises would presumably lie, see section 9, Trade Union Act 1871). Whether or not an injunction will be granted to restrain a trade union from committing a tort in the future has not yet been finally determined, the dicta on this point being conflicting: see *Ware & De Freville* v. *Motor Trade Association* (1921), *Boulting* v. *A.C.T.A.T.* (1963), and *Torquay Hotel Co.* v. *Cousins* (1968).

IMMUNITY OF TRADE UNION OFFICIALS AND WORKMEN. Certain protections are given if an act is done "in furtherance or contemplation of a trade dispute". The expression "trade dispute" means "any dispute between employers and workmen, or between workmen and workmen, which is connected with the employment or non-employment, or the terms of employment, or with the conditions of labour, of any person ..." (s. 5, Trade Disputes Act 1906).

Thus a dispute between employers is not a trade dispute: *Larkin* v. *Long* (1915). A trade dispute does not exist if it is merely inter-union rivalry: *Stratford* v. *Lindley* (1964), but it does exist if the union is trying to obtain recognition in order to promote the interests of its members.

Beetham v, *Trinidad Cement Ltd.* (1960)

A trade union sought recognition from a company in order to bargain on behalf of its members who were employed there.

Held, a trade dispute existed. The union was acting on behalf of its members, and therefore there was a difference between the employers and workmen.

There is not a trade dispute if the union officials are pursuing their own personal grudge (*Huntley* v. *Thornton* (*ante*)), or if there is no industrial quarrel with the employer in question.

Torquay Hotel v. *Cousins* (1968)

The T. & G. W. Union was in dispute with several hotels. A director of the plaintiff company (which was not involved in the dispute), made a statement which so incensed the union that a dispute with the plaintiff's hotel was declared.

Held, there was no trade dispute. None of the employees of the plaintiff were members of the union, and there was no dispute as to their conditions of employment.

The "act" must be "in furtherance or contemplation of" the trade dispute for it to come within the statutory protections; thus if a trade dispute exists, but the act is not done in furtherance of it, but for some other reason, the protection will not be available.

Conway v. *Wade* (1909)

The defendant informed the plaintiff's employers that unless the plaintiff was dismissed a strike would take place. This was not true, but the defendant's action was done in order to force the plaintiff to pay an outstanding fine.

Held, although there was a trade dispute, the act was not done in furtherance of that dispute, but for other motives.

To obtain information which, after consideration, may lead to a dispute does not mean that the dispute is already in existence: *Bents Brewery* v. *Hogan* (1945).

If the act is done in furtherance or contemplation of a trade dispute, the following protections arise:

(a) Section 1, Trade Disputes Act 1906. An act shall not be actionable as a conspiracy, unless the act would be actionable if done by an individual. In *Rookes* v. *Barnard*, it was thought that this section applied only in those circumstances where the workmen were pursuing personal grudges, rather than legitimate trade union activities. (But since in these circumstances it cannot be said that a trade dispute exists, it seems that the House of Lords confined it to an area where it cannot normally arise!). However, tha fact that the workmen are influenced by spite does not take them out of the statutory protection if otherwise they are within it.

Dallimore v. *Williams* (1914)

A trade union official brought a band out on strike in order to secure higher wages. There was evidence of strong personal animosity between the official and the band-master.

Held, a trade dispute existed.

(b) Section 3, Trade Disputes Act 1906. An act shall not be actionable on the ground only that ("*Limb* 1)" it induces some other person to break a contract of employment, or ("*Limb* 2") it is an interference with the trade, business or profession of another person. It should be noted that *Limb* 1 only protects the inducement of the breach of a contract of employment. *Limb* 2, on the other hand, does *not* protect the inducement of a breach of a commercial contract (*Stratford* v. *Lindley—ante*). Further, since the whole section applies "only" if these specific torts are alleged, it has no relevance if there is some other heading of liability, such as intimidation.

(c) Section 1 Trade Disputes Act 1965. An act shall not be actionable on the ground only that it consists of a person threatening that a contract of employment will be broken, or that he will induce another to break a contract of employment. The purpose of this section was to give a limited protection to trade union officials who were placed in jeopardy as a result of *Rookes* v. *Barnard* (*supra*).

4. Picketing

By section 2 of the Trade Disputes Act 1906, picketing is lawful if it is

   (a) peaceful,

   (b) solely for the purpose of either obtaining or communicating information or persuading people to work or not to work,

   (c) done in furtherance or contemplation of a trade dispute.

The picketing can only take place at or near, not in, the premises where a person resides or works or carries on business. But if a police constable apprehends that there may be a breach of the peace, he may lawfully restrict the number of pickets who may be placed at the premises: *Piddington* v. *Bates* (1960). Moreover, pickets are not entitled to obstruct the highway.

Tynan v. *Balmer* (1966)

   Forty pickets walked in a circle in a road near the entrance to a factory where there was a dispute. The object was to bring traffic to a standstill.

   Held, the obstruction of the highway constituted a nuisance, which was not authorised by the 1906 Act.

It will be a criminal offence to use violence, intimidation, to persistently follow, hide any tools or property, watch and beset the house or works of a person, etc.: Conspiracy and Protection of Property Act 1875, s. 7).

5. Criminal Liability for Strikes

1. THE CONSPIRACY AND PROTECTION OF PROPERTY ACT 1875 creates two criminal offences in connection with strike activities.

(i) Section 4. It is a criminal offence for a person employed in the connection with the supply of gas or water to *break* his contract of employment, knowing or having reasonable cause to believe that the probable consequence of his act, whether done alone or in combination with others, will deprive persons of the supply of gas or water. This provision was extended to the supply of electricity by the Electricity (Supply) Act 1919.

(ii) Section 5. It is also a criminal offence for a person to *break* his contract of employment, the probable consequence of which is to endanger human life, or cause serious bodily injury, or to expose valuable property to destruction or injury.

In either case, however, there is nothing to prevent employees from terminating their contracts of employment.

2. THE POLICE ACT 1964 provides that it shall be a criminal offence to do anything likely to cause disaffection, breach of discipline, or the withdrawal of labour of members of the police force. Police are forbidden to join trade unions, but may belong to the Police Federation.

3. THE MERCHANT SHIPPING ACT 1894 laid down a comprehensive code governing merchant seamen. They are forbidden to strike without terminating their contracts of employment, and incitement to strike may amount to a criminal offence.

4. THE POST OFFICE ACT 1953 provides that any person who wilfully hinders the progress of mail may be guilty of a criminal offence.

6. The Settlement of Industrial Disputes

Since British industrial relations is based essentially on a voluntary system, there are no compulsory powers which would enable the State to interfere in such a dispute. (See, however, Terms and Conditions of Employment Act 1959, *supra* p. 62). There are, however, four methods whereby the State can play a role.

(a) CONCILIATION—Where a dispute exists between employers and workmen, the Minister may

(i) enquire into the causes of the dispute

(ii) take steps to enable the parties to meet under the chairmanship of a person nominated by him or otherwise mutually agreed

(iii) at the request of one of the parties, he may appoint a conciliator: Conciliation Act, 1896.

(b) ARBITRATION—Where a dispute exists or is apprehended, the Minister may, if both parties agree

(i) refer the matter to the Industrial Court for settlement

(ii) refer the matter for settlement to an arbitrator or a board of arbitrators: Industrial Court Act 1919; Conciliation Act 1896.

A reference to arbitration is only remitted if there has been a failure to settle the dispute by existing procedural arrangements. The resultant arbitration awards are not legally binding.

(c) COURT OF ENQUIRY—Where a trade dispute exists or is

apprehended, the Minister may appoint a Court of Enquiry to investigate the causes of the dispute, and its report is submitted to Parliament by the Minister. Although it has no legal force, it is a useful way of getting an independent view on the dispute, and its suggestions for a settlement are usually adopted: Industrial Courts Act 1919.

(d) COMMITTEE OF INVESTIGATION—This is a less formal method than the Court of Enquiry, and its report does not have to be published: Conciliation Act 1896.

7. Permanent Institutions

(i) INDUSTRIAL COURT—The Court was created by the Act of 1919, and is composed of a President (having the status of a High Court Judge) and a number of persons representing both sides of industry. The Court is not a Court of law, but a permanent arbitration tribunal, and exercises its functions in a private arbitral fashion (R. v. *Industrial Court, ex parte A.S.S.E.T.* 1964). The Court sits in divisions with an independent chairman and a representative of employers and employees respectively. There are a number of statutes which empower the Minister to refer certain disputes to the Court (e.g. Road Haulage Wages Act 1938, Civil Aviation Act 1946).

(ii) COMMISSION FOR INDUSTRIAL RELATIONS—This body was established as a result of the Royal Commission of Trade Unions and Employers' Associations, and its present existence depends on a Royal Commission, pending statutory confirmation. The Secretary of State may refer specific points to the Commission for study, in particular, disputes procedures in industry.

(iii) INDUSTRIAL TRIBUNALS—Created by the Industrial Training Act 1964, a tribunal consists of a legally qualified Chairman and a representative of employers and trade unions respectively. Decisions are reached by a majority vote. The tribunals have jurisdiction to hear and determine matters which arise out of

    (a) Contracts of Employment Act 1963
    (b) Industrial Training Act 1964
    (c) Redundancy Payments Act 1965
    (d) Selective Employment Payments Act 1966
    (e) Other miscellaneous legislation.

Chapter 5 *Industrial Insurance*

Two compulsory schemes enable certain benefits to be paid to the insured person on the occurrence of certain specified contingencies. The relevant legislation is (i) the National Insurance Act 1965, and (ii) the National Insurance (Industrial Injuries) Act 1965.

1. National Insurance Act 1965

For the purpose of the Act, insured persons are either

  (a) employed (i.e. those engaged under a contract of service)
  (b) self-employed (i.e. those who engage in contracts for services)
  (c) non-employed.

Any disputes as to which category a particular person should be placed in must be referred to the Minister by the Local Insurance Officer, and an appeal lies to the High Court from his decisions. Certain persons are exempt from making contributions to the scheme, though they may still be entitled to receive benefits; these are

  (a) Married Women
  (b) Full-time students
  (c) Persons whose income is less than a certain minimum
  (d) Unemployed persons and those who are medically unfit for work.

There are eight benefits which are payable under the Scheme:

  (1) UNEMPLOYMENT BENEFIT—The first three days of a person's unemployment are known as "waiting days". Benefit is not payable in respect of these three days, unless the claimant is unemployed

F

for a further nine days during the period of thirteen weeks. Flat-rate unemployment benefit is payable for 312 days, and in addition, an earnings related supplement may be payable for 156 days.

Disqualification from benefits. (a) A worker will not get benefit if he is out of work as a result of a trade dispute, unless he can show (i) that he is not taking part in it, or financing it, or is interested in it, and (ii) that he was not, prior to the dispute, of the same grade or class of worker involved in the dispute. The Insurance Officer need only show that the worker is unemployed because of a stoppage due to a trade dispute, and the onus is then on the claimant to show that he is entitled to benefit under one of the exceptions.

(b) He may be disqualified for up to six weeks if he lost his job through industrial misconduct, or left without just cause. He may similarly be disqualified if he refuses to accept suitable employment offered to him, or neglected to make himself available for employment. Employment is *not* suitable if the situation is vacant because of a trade dispute or if the wages offered are lower than the rate generally observed by good employers, or less favourable than the terms of a collective agreement.

2. SICKNESS BENEFIT—If the claimant has made more than 156 payments into the scheme, he can claim on appropriate medical grounds for an indefinite period. If less than 156 contributions have been paid, sickness benefit is payable for 312 days. Earnings—related supplement commences on the 13th day of illness, and continues for 156 days.

3. RETIREMENT PENSION
4. MATERNITY BENEFIT
5. WIDOW'S BENEFIT
6. GUARDIAN'S ALLOWANCES
7. CHILD'S SPECIAL ALLOWANCE
8. DEATH GRANT

2. National Insurance (Industrial Injuries) Act 1965

All persons employed in insurable employment are insured against

(i) personal injury caused by accident arising out of and in the course of their employment

(ii) against prescribed diseases or prescribed personal injury not so caused but being an injury or disease due to the nature of the employment.

PERSONAL INJURY, includes mental, as well as physical injury (*Yates* v. *South Kirby Collieries* 1910).

The following interpretations must be born in mind:

Caused by accident An accident is an "untoward event, which is not expected or designed": *Fenton* v. *Thorley & Co* (1903). Thus the wilful act of a third party may be an accident, as will be an injury caused by skylarking, or someone else's negligence. A series of events may be an accident if they result in a physiological change for the worse in the condition of the claimant, and that change was substantially induced by the work upon which he was engaged.

Arising out of the employment—To arise out of the employment, the accident must have occurred while the claimant was doing something that he was employed to do, or reasonably incidental to it. Thus unauthorised acts may disqualify a person from benefit, as will certain common risks.

In the course of the employment—This refers to the time element, i.e., the accident must occur after the commencement of the employment, and before its termination. If an accident occurs in the course of the employment, there is a presumption that it also *arises out of* that employment, though this presumption is capable of being rebutted: R. v. *National Insurance Commissioner, ex parte Richardson* (1958).

CERTAIN SPECIAL CIRCUMSTANCES REQUIRE CONSIDERATION:

(a) *Travelling to work.* An accident which occurs while the claimant is travelling, with the express or implied permission of the employer, as a passenger in any vehicle to and from his work shall, not withstanding that the claimant is under no obligation to use that transport, be deemed to have arisen out of and in the course of the employment if

(1) the accident would be so deemed had there been such an obligation, and
(2) the transport is being operated by the employer or some other person on his behalf, and is not being operated in the course of public transport: s. 8.

(b) *Acting in an emergency*—An accident which occurs while the claimant is in or about any premises at which he is for the time being employed shall be deemed to have arisen out of his employment if it happens while he is taking steps on an actual or supposed emergency to rescue or protect persons who are, or thought to be, injured, or to minimise serious damage to property: s. 9.

(c) *Disobeying orders*—If an accident occurs while the claimant is acting contrary to any statutory or other regulation, or contrary to orders given by or on behalf of the employer, it shall still be deemed to have arisen in the course of his employment, if (1) the accident would have been deemed to have arisen has there been no such contravention, and (2) he acted for the purpose of and in connection with his employers business: s. 7.

PRESCRIBED INDUSTRIAL DISEASES AND INJURIES:

The Minister has power to list the diseases and injuries which are covered by the Act, and can extend this list if he is satisfied that

(a) it ought to be treated as a risk of the occupation, and

(b) it is attributed to the special nature of the employment.

To claim benefit, the claimant must show (1) that he has contracted the prescribed disease, or suffered the prescribed injury, (2) that he has been employed in the occupation stated to be responsible for that disease, and (3) that the contracting of the disease or injury was due to the occupation. (There is a presumption to this effect, but this is capable of being rebutted).

BENEFITS PAYABLE UNDER THE SCHEME

(a) Injury benefit. This is payable for every day the insured is incapable of work (excluding Sundays) for a maximum period of 156 days. No payment is made for the first three days, unless the incapacity lasts for at least 12 days.

(b) Industrial disablement benefit. This is a payment made according to the degree of disability, and may be claimed even though the claimant is not absent from work. The disability need not be substantial or permanent, and it includes disfigurement. The benefit may be paid as a lump sum, or a weekly pension.

(c) Death benefit.

(d) Unemployment supplement.

(e) Special hardship cases.
(f) Constant attendance allowance.
(g) Hospital treatment.
(h) Dependants' allowance.

Index